Pleasures from the Good Earth

A Collection of Recipes
by the
Lakewood Ranch Women's Club, Inc.
and the
Residents of Lakewood Ranch

Copyright © 2000
Cookbooks by Morris Press

Printed in the U.S.A. by
Cookbooks by Morris Press
P.O. Box 2110 • Kearney, NE 68848

For information on having your cookbook printed, write for
our FREE information packet or call Toll-Free at 1-800-445-6621.

34808-mu   1

Introduction

The Lakewood Ranch Women's Club was founded in 1997 by a small group of energetic Lakewood Ranch residents chaired by Elizabeth Norton. At that time, there were fewer than 500 homes built in this new master-planned community carved from the beautiful Schroeder-Manatee Ranch. In this year 2000, the Ranch will have become home to 2000 families, who have come from all over the United States and from other countries in the world; and our Club has grown along with it.

The purpose of the Club is to create friendship and support among members of the Lakewood Ranch community by presenting programs serving the interests of women today, by contributing to civic responsibilities and charitable causes, and by fostering growth and friendship among our members. We are a not-for-profit service club founded to improve the quality of life in our community.

We are fortunate to live in this lovely community with its lakes, parks, walking trails, golf courses, and many amenities. We hope you take pleasure in the recipes and in the thought that the profits will go to charity and help contribute to the quality of life for those who are not so fortunate.

Jo Anne Dain, President

Dedication

To our Past Presidents, who devoted their time and energy to help create our organization:

Elizabeth Norton, 1997
Karen Michener, 1998
Jane Drake, 1999

Acknowledgments

We would like to acknowledge and gratefully thank all those who worked to make this cookbook a reality, including:

Our wonderful contributors whose recipes made this book possible.

The Lakewood Ranch Women's Club Cookbook Committee, chaired by Lorraine Mondulick, who spent countless hours collecting, sorting, and proofing the recipes.

The Community Services Office and the Courtside Deli at the Athletic Club for distributing forms and collecting recipes.

Schroeder-Manatee Ranch for their support.

And thanks to all of you who have purchased a book and contributed with your dollars to the success of this project.

Lakewood Ranch Women's Club

Lakewood Ranch Women's Club

P.O. Box 21286
Bradenton, FL 34304
(941) 756-5689

2000 Officers

Jo Anne Dain, President
Angela Smith, Vice-President
Virginia Orenstein, Treasurer
Shirley Cote, Recording Secretary
Ellen Grabowski, Corresponding Secretary

Cookbook Committee

Lorraine Mondulick, Chair
Helen Cueto
Ellen Grabowski
Judy Grant
Jane Goodrich
Barbara Grossman
Maria Hutchinson
Marie Scott
Phyllis Troy
Jan Winn

Table of Contents

Appetizers & Beverages

Helpful Hints

- You won't need sugar with your tea if you drink jasmine tea or any of the lighter-bodied varieties, like Formosa Oolong, which have their own natural sweetness. They are fine for sugarless iced tea, too.

- Calorie-free club soda adds sparkle to iced fruit juices, makes them go further and reduces calories per portion.

- For tea flavoring, dissolve old-fashioned lemon drops or hard mint candy in your tea. They melt quickly and keep the tea brisk!

- Most diets call for 8 ounces of milk and 4 ounces of fruit juice. Check your glassware. Having the exact size glass ensures the correct serving amount.

- Make your own spiced tea or cider. Place orange peels, whole cloves, and cinnamon sticks in a 6-inch square piece of cheesecloth. Gather the corners and tie with a string. Steep in hot cider or tea for 10 minutes or longer if you want a stronger flavor.

- Always chill juices or sodas before adding to beverage recipes.

- To cool your punch, float an ice ring made from the punch rather than using ice cubes. Not only is this more decorative, but it also inhibits melting and diluting.

- Place fresh or dried mint in the bottom of a cup of hot chocolate for a cool and refreshing taste.

- One lemon yields about ¼ cup juice; one orange yields about ⅓ cup juice. This is helpful in making fresh orange juice or lemonade!

- Never boil coffee; it brings out the acid and causes a bitter taste. Store ground coffee in the refrigerator or freezer to keep it fresh.

- Always use COLD water for electric drip coffee makers. Use 1 to 2 tablespoons ground coffee for each cup of water.

- Seeds and nuts, both shelled and unshelled, keep best and longest when stored in the freezer. Unshelled nuts crack more easily when frozen. Nuts and seeds can be used directly from the freezer.

- Cheeses should be served at room temperature, approximately 70°.

Appetizers & Beverages

DELICIOUS CHICKEN WINGS FOR PARTIES

Ethel Rudy

4 lbs. chicken wingettes
1 c. Parmesan cheese
½ c. butter
2 T. parsley flakes

1 tsp. oregano
1 tsp. salt
½ tsp. pepper
2 tsp. paprika

Melt butter in pan; dip wingettes into the melted butter. Blend cheese, parsley flakes, oregano, salt, pepper and paprika; roll wingettes in the mixture. Arrange in a glass baking dish. Bake at 350° for 1 hour.

HOOTER'S BUFFALO CHICKEN WINGS

Linda Kammerer

Vegetable oil for frying
¼ c. butter
¼ c. hot sauce
Dash ground pepper
Dash of garlic powder

½ c. all-purpose flour
¼ tsp. paprika
¼ tsp. cayenne pepper
¼ tsp. salt
10 chicken wing pieces

Heat oil in deep fryer to 375°. (Use enough oil and cover wings entirely, approximately 1 inch deep). Combine butter, hot sauce, ground pepper and garlic powder in a small saucepan over low heat. Heat until butter is melted and ingredients are well blended. Combine flour, paprika, cayenne pepper and salt in a small bowl. If wings are frozen, defrost and dry them. Put wings into a large bowl and sprinkle flour mixture over them, coating each wing evenly. Put wings in refrigerator 60 to 90 minutes (helps breading stick). Put all the wings into the hot oil and fry them for 10 to 15 minutes or until some parts of the wings begin to turn brown. Place wings on paper towel to drain, then place in large bowl. Add hot sauce and stir to coat wings.

CHORIZO WITH WINE

Barbara Grossman

2 links chorizo sausage
1-2 T. olive oil
2 T. chopped garlic

¼ c. dry white wine
1 T. chopped fresh parsley

Slice chorizo diagonally and place in a heavy dry skillet. Sauté until browned. Add a little olive and the garlic; continue to cook until garlic is golden. Deglaze pan carefully with the wine, then add parsley. Cook slow 10 to 15 minutes longer, adding more wine, if needed. Serve with thinly sliced Italian bread.

SUE'S ITALIAN SQUARES

Lorraine Mondulick

¼ lb. provolone, sliced thin
¼ lb. Swiss cheese, sliced thin
¼ lb. boiled ham, sliced thin
¼ lb. salami, sliced thin
¼ lb. pepperoni, sliced thin

3 lg. eggs
1 sm. jar roasted red peppers
1 sm. can black olives, sliced
2 pkgs. crescent rolls
13 x 9-inch pan

Roll out 1 package crescent rolls on the bottom of pan. Layer meat and cheese, then olives and peppers. Beat eggs and pour over meat and cheese. Roll second package crescent rolls. Place on top of meat. Bake at 350° for 30 minutes. Let rest, then slice, into squares small enough for appetizers.

PARTY RYE APPETIZERS

Pauline Bridge

Brown lightly:

1 lb. ground beef

1 lb. sausage

Pour off grease.

Add:

1 tsp. red pepper flakes
1 tsp. oregano

½ tsp. garlic salt
1 lb. Velveeta cheese, cubed

60 slices round party rye

Brown meat, pour off grease. Add spices and cheese; cut into cubes. Put on party rye slices. Freeze on cookie sheets, covered. **To serve:** Thaw slightly and broil 5 minutes or bubbly. Serves 60.

SWEET AND SOUR MEATBALLS

Shirley Cote
Rhonda Maule

1 lb. ground beef
½ c. bread crumbs
1 tsp. salt
⅛ tsp. pepper
1 egg

½ tsp. Worcestershire sauce
¼ c. milk
1 T. parsley
1 (12-oz.) bottle chili sauce
1 (10-oz.) jar grape jelly

Mix ground beef, bread crumbs, salt, pepper, egg, Worcestershire sauce, milk and parsley; roll into firm meatballs. Brown in oil and drain. One-half hour before serving, heat chili sauce and grape jelly. Add meatballs and simmer uncovered for 30 minutes so sauce thickens and coats meatballs. Do not use crockpot!

2

34808-00

"YIDDISH" CHRISTMAS MEATBALLS

Leslie McQueen

2 lbs. lean ground beef	2 tsp. garlic powder
1 minced onion	1 bottle chili sauce
2 eggs	¼ bottle water
½ c. crushed cornflakes	6-oz. jar grape jelly
½ tsp. salt	1 T. lemon juice

Mix ground beef, minced onion, 2 eggs, cornflakes, salt and garlic powder; form into bite-size meatballs. Combine chili sauce, water, grape jelly and lemon juice in a saucepan on low flame. Heat until jelly melts. Drop in meatballs, cover and allow to simmer slowly for about 45 minutes.

ONION TART

Diane Neal

2 c. sliced sweet onions	Salt & pepper
2 T. butter	1 egg
1 can crescent rolls	¼ c. evaporated milk

Preheat oven to 400°. Sauté onion in butter until golden and tender. Separate rolls into triangles. Place in ungreased 8-inch pie plate, overlapping as necessary and pressing together to form even crust on the bottom and half way up sides. Spread onion over dough. Salt and pepper. Beat egg slightly, stir in milk. Pour egg mixture over onions. Bake 20 to 25 minutes or until crust is golden. Cut into wedges. Serve hot or room temperature.

COOL VEGGIE PIZZA

Judith Grant

1 (8-oz.) can refrigerated crescent rolls	1½ tsp. mayonnaise
1 (0-oz.) pkg. cream cheese, softened	1 T. dill weed

Toppings (optional):

Chopped zucchini	Carrot sprouts
Onions	Garlic
Broccoli	Peppers
Mozzarella cheese	Cheddar cheese
Mushrooms	Olives
Tomatoes	

Set oven to 350°. Spread roll dough on round pizza rack, pinch seams together. Bake until lightly brown. Remove from oven and cool. Blend together cream cheese, mayonnaise and dill weed. Spread cheese

(continued)

mixture on top of cold crust. Finely chop all toppings. Sprinkle a layer of each over crust. Garnish with grated mozzarella cheese, cheddar cheese. Refrigerate. Cut in pizza wedges. Serve.

Variation: Mexican: Mix cream cheese with 2 tablespoons sour cream, 2 tablespoons taco seasoning mix. Omit mayonnaise and dill weed. Use shredded lettuce, green onions, olives, cheddar cheese and tomatoes.

CAVIAR PIE

Michelle James

6 hard-boiled eggs
3 T. mayonnaise
1½ c. chopped Bermuda (red) onion
8 oz. softened cream cheese
⅔ c. sour cream

4.7 oz. black or red lumpfish caviar (the supermarket variety)
Optional garnish: Lemon parsley, capers, crackers, thin bread or toasted

Grease well an 8-or 9-inch springform pan. Chop 6 hard-boiled eggs, combine with mayonnaise and spread over pan. Sprinkle with chopped onion. Blend softened cream cheese with sour cream and spread over onion. Cover and chill 3 hours. Just before serving, top with black or red caviar. Remove sides of springform pan. Garnish with lemon, parsley, capers as desired. Serve with knife or spreader on side, so people can spread caviar pie on crackers or toast.

CRISFIELD'S CRAB IMPERIAL

Michelle James

1 lb. lump crab meat, picked over for shell
½ c. green bell pepper, minced
¼ c. onion, minced

¾ c. mayonnaise
3 T. butter, melted
½ c. fresh bread crumbs

Combine the crab meat, peppers and onion; gently fold in the mayonnaise. Mold the mixture into a clean crab shell or other heatproof serving dish and cover with melted butter and bread crumbs. Bake at 350° for 12 minutes or until crumbs are golden brown. Serve at once.

CRAB OR SHRIMP DELIGHT

Roberta Barbaro

1 (6-oz.) pkg. cream cheese
½ c. chopped green onion
1 c. salad dressing
1 c. chopped celery

1 c. cream of mushroom soup
1 env. gelatin
1 sm. can crab or shrimp, drained

Combine cream cheese, green onion, salad dressing and celery. Heat mushroom soup and dissolve gelatin in it. Combine all ingredients and

(continued)

4

34808-00

add drained crab or shrimp. Pour into mold and refrigerate until solid. Serve with crackers.

SHRIMP AND CRAB MOLD

Lorraine Mondulick

1 can tomato soup, undiluted
1/4 c. cold water
2 pkgs. unflavored gelatin
2 (8-oz.) pkgs. cream cheese
1/2 c. finely diced onion
1 c. finely diced celery

2 cans tiny shrimp
1 c. crab meat (imitation) or real, diced
Dill weed
Onion powder
White pepper to taste

Dissolve gelatin in cold water in separate pan. Bring soup to a boil. Add dissolved gelatin to soup and stir. Add cream cheese. Simmer until cheese melts. If lumpy, beat with beater until smooth. Remove from heat. Add remaining ingredients. Stir and pour into sprayed mold or pretty dish. Set for 2 hours or until firm. Serve with crackers.

DILLED SHRIMP

Jane Stanton

1 1/2 c. mayonnaise
1/3 c. lemon juice
1/4 c. sugar
1/4 tsp. salt

1/2 c. sour cream
1 thinly sliced red onion
2 T. dill
3 lbs. shrimp, cooked & shelled

Mix mayonnaise, lemon juice, sugar, salt, sour cream, red onion and dill. Add the shrimp and marinate for 24 hours before serving.

SHRIMP DIP

Donna Arakel

1 can tiny shrimp
2 "heaping" T. mayonnaise

1 (8-oz.) bar cream cheese
1 sm. onion

Place drained shrimp in bowl and crush finely with fork. Soften cream cheese and add to shrimp along with mayonnaise. Cut small onion up very finely and add to mixture. Mix all ingredients together and place in serving dish in refrigerator for 1/2 hour. Serve with crackers.

SHRIMP DIP

Leslie McQueen

1 can sm. shrimp
8 oz. cream cheese
1/2 c. mayonnaise
1/2 grated onion

2 T. chili sauce
2 T. lemon juice
1 tsp. sugar
Salt & pepper to taste

(continued)

Add all ingredients together. Refrigerate for at least 1 to 2 hours. Serve with crackers.

CHUNKY CLAM AND BACON DIP WITH PARSLEY PITA TOASTS

Barbara Grossman

¼ lb. bacon, chopped
2 (6½-oz.) cans minced clams
8 oz. cream cheese, softened
¼ c. sour cream
⅓ c. finely chopped red bell
   pepper
3 scallions, chopped fine

2 T. finely chopped fresh basil
1 tsp. drained bottled
   horseradish
1 tsp. fresh lemon juice
¾ tsp. Worcestershire sauce
Tabasco to taste
Pita toasts, accompaniment

In a skillet cook bacon over moderate heat, stirring, until golden and crisp. Transfer with slotted spoon to paper towel to drain. In a large sieve, set over a bowl, drain clams, reserving clam juice and in another bowl whisk together cream cheese and sour cream. Whisk 2 tablespoons reserved clam juice into cream cheese mixture with clams, bacon and remaining ingredients. (May be made one day ahead, cover and chill.) Bring to room temperature before serving. Makes 2 cups.

Parsley Pita Toasts:

1 (12-oz.) pkg. pita bread, cut
   into wedges
¼ c. chopped fresh parsley

3 T. olive oil
2 T. chopped finely green onion

Preheat oven to 350°. Place pita wedges on baking sheet. Mix parsley, olive oil and green onions in small bowl; brush over pita wedges. Bake until crisp, about 15 to 20 minutes. Cool. (Can be prepared day ahead. Store in airtight container, at room temperature. Serves 8 to 10.

CLAM SPREAD

Valarie Grimwood

1 stick butter or margarine
1½ tubes Ritz crackers

1 can Gortons minced clams
1 sm. onion

Melt butter. Crush Ritz crackers and add to butter. Mix until well coated. Add chopped onion and clams and the juice. Mix and bake at 350° for 30 minutes. Spread on Ritz crackers or any plain crackers.

34808-00

PAPA HARRYS' CHEESE KNISHES

Helen Cueto

3 pkgs. crescent rolls
½ lb. farmers cheese
½ lb. cream cheese
1 egg

1 c. diced onion
2 T. butter, melted
1 tsp. sugar
Pinch of salt

Sauté onion in butter. Mix farmers cheese, cream cheese and egg. Add to onion. Add sugar and salt. Cut crescent rolls in half. Place a heaping teaspoon on the wide of each wedge and roll from the wide end. Bake on ungreased cookie sheet until golden, 12 to 15 minutes in a 350° oven. May be frozen.

CHEESE BALL

Pauline Bridge

1 (8 oz.) Philadelphia cream
  cheese
1 Jar bacon cheese
3 T. bleu cheese
Dash Worcestershire sauce

Dash salt
Dash garlic salt
Dash seasoned salt
Butter milk or sour cream to
  thin

Soften and mix all ingredients. Thin with buttermilk or sour cream. Form into ball or log. Cover with ground nuts, if desired.

CHEESE PUFFS

Leslie McQueen

1 lg. (8-oz.) pkg. cream cheese
1 egg yolk
1 lg. pinch baking powder

1 tsp. onion powder
4 T. minced mushrooms
1 sm. can shredded crab

Blend all ingredients together. Spread mixture onto small rye bread rounds. Bake at 450° for about 8 minutes.

CHEESE DIP

Angela Smith

3 c. Swiss, grated
3 c. cheddar, grated

6 c. onion, chopped
6 c. mayonnaise

Mix Swiss, cheddar, onion and mayonnaise. Place in baking dish. Bake 1 hour at 350°. Serve on crackers.

DORIS' CHEESE SPREAD

Jocelyn Stevens

1 block Velveeta	4 oz. horseradish
½ c. mayonnaise	

Melt Velveeta in microwave. Add mayonnaise and horseradish. Chill and serve with crackers.

CHEESE QUESO

Susan Hickman

1 sm. box Velveeta cheese	4 chopped fresh jalapeños
1 can Ro-Tel tomatoes (hot or regular)	2 T. chopped cilantro
½ c. chopped onion	½ lb. sausage, cooked (opt.)

Place all ingredients in a crockpot or double boiler until smooth and creamy, stirring often. Serve with tortilla chips or warm flour tortillas for dipping. You can also add ½ pound cooked Italian sausage.

CHEESE-CHILI APPETIZER

Audrey Millican

½ c. butter	1 pt. cottage cheese
10 eggs or EggBeaters	1 lb. Jack cheese with jalapeño peppers, grated
½ c. flour	
1 tsp. baking powder	2 T. chopped jalapeños (opt.)
1 (8-oz.) can chopped green chilies	

Melt butter in a 13 x 9 x 2-inch Pyrex dish. Beat eggs lightly in large bowl. Add flour, baking powder, green chilies, cottage cheese, Jack cheese and jalapeños. Mix until just blended. Pour batter into buttered Pyrex dish. Bake at 400° for 15 minutes. Reduce heat to 350° and bake 35 of 40 minutes longer. Cut in bite-size squares and serve hot.

TACO DIP

Maria Hutchinson

1 (8 oz.) softened cream cheese	2 tomatoes, diced
1 (8-oz.) jar salsa	4 c. shredded cheddar/Monterey Jack cheese
1 clove garlic, minced	
Half head shredded lettuce	

Assemble on a large plate or platter. Spread softened mixture of cream cheese/salsa mixture. (Add minced garlic, if needed.) Layer with shredded lettuce, cheese and diced tomatoes. Serve with nacho chips.

34808-00

TACO CASSEROLE

Darlene Jenny

1 lb. lean ground beef
1 env. dry taco seasoning mix
1 (15.5-oz.) can dark red kidney
  beans, drained
⅔ head iceberg lettuce, torn or
  shredded
2 onions, chopped
2 lg. or 3 med. tomatoes,
  chopped

2 c. (8 oz.) grated cheese
  (Monterey Jack, Cheddar or a
  combination)
1 (8-oz.) bottle creamy French
  salad dressing
1 bag Doritos nacho cheese
  chips, crushed

Cook and stir ground beef in a large skillet until it loses its red color. Drain. Toss with one-half of the dry taco seasoning mix. Combine the remaining dry taco seasoning mix with the drained kidney beans. In a 13 x 9-inch glass rectangular dish assemble ingredients in order. Distribute torn or shredded lettuce on the bottom. Sprinkle chopped onion on top of the lettuce. Next is the browned and seasoned ground beef. Seasoned kidney beans in the next layer. Then sprinkle chopped tomatoes on top of kidney beans. Over all goes the shredded cheese. Finally, spread the creamy French salad dressing over the top.

SUPER SUPPER DIP

Suzi Massey

1½ lbs. ground beef
½ c. chopped onion
16 oz. refried beans
4 oz. diced green chilies
8 oz. salsa

8 oz. shredded cheddar cheese
1 c. sour cream
⅓ c. chopped green onion
¼ c. chopped black olives
Tortilla chips

Heat oven to 350°. Cook and stir beef and onions until beef is brown; drain. Spoon ½ beans into greased 13 x 9-inch pan. Top with ½ each of beef, chilies, salsa and cheese. Repeat with remaining beans, beef, chilies, salsa and cheese. Bake 30 minutes. Top with sour cream, green onions and olives. Serve with chips. Serves 6.

CURRY DIP

Leslie McQueen

1½ c. mayonnaise
2 tsp. curry powder
1 T. grated onion
½ tsp. dry mustard

½ tsp. salt
⅛ tsp. black pepper
Dash of Tabasco

Mix all ingredients. Chill thoroughly. Use with fresh vegetables or as a dip for fish instead of tartar sauce.

AVOCADO DIP

Nancy Gonzalez

½ sm. onion, finely chopped
2 serrano chilies, stemmed, seeded & finely chopped
1 med. tomato, finely chopped
1 clove garlic, peeled & finely chopped

8 sprigs cilantro, finely chopped
3 ripe, med. avocados (Hass)
½ tsp. salt
½ c. lime juice

In a medium-size bowl, mix finely chopped onion and chilies with tomato, garlic and cilantro. Cut the avocados lengthwise. Loosen the meat from the pits, then scoop out the pits and reserve. Scrape the avocado pulp from the skins and add it to the bowl. Using a fork or spoon, roughly mash the avocados while mixing in the other ingredients: chiles, tomato, garlic, cilantro, salt and lime juice. Return pits to the guacamole and cover with plastic wrap. Set aside a few minutes to let flavors blend.

GREEN CHILIES DIP

Valarie Grimwood

1 (4-oz.) can chopped green chilies
1 (8½-oz.) can artichoke hearts

1 c. low fat mayonnaise
1 c. grated Parmesan cheese

Drain and chop artichoke hearts. Drain green chilies. Add mayonnaise and cheese. Mix well and pour into a shallow 8-inch serving dish. Bake at 325° for 20 to 25 minutes or until golden brown crust forms. Serve with plain tortilla chips or Fritos.

DILL VEGETABLE DIP

Mary Button

⅔ c. mayonnaise
⅔ c. sour cream
1 T. dill weed
1 T. parsley flakes

1 T. dried shredded green onion flakes
1 tsp. beau monde seasoning

Blend together mayonnaise and sour cream. Add remaining ingredients and blend well. Makes 1½ cups.

ARTICHOKE DIP

Shirley Grube

2 cans artichoke hearts, drained
4 oz. mayonnaise
⅓ c. Parmesan cheese

Bread crumbs
Melted butter

(continued)

34808-00

Mix artichokes, mayonnaise and Parmesan cheese. Put into 8-inch pie pan; sprinkle bread crumbs on top. Drizzle lightly with melted butter. Bake at 350° for about 30 minutes. Serve with crackers.

TAMPENADE

Michelle James

1 can ripe olives (black), pitted	3 T. olive oil
6 Greek olives (remove pit)	Plenty of black pepper
1 lg. clove garlic	anchovie oil
3 T. capers	

Chop garlic in food processor. Add olives and chop coarsely. Add capers, oil and blend to a mealy consistency. (Add more oil, if needed.) Keeps several weeks in a refrigerator.

ROASTED PEPPER AND ARTICHOKE TAPENADE

Andrea Junghans

1 (7-oz.) jar roasted bell pepper, drained, coarsely chopped	1/2 c. freshly grated Parmesan cheese
1 (6-oz.) jar marinated artichoke, drained & coarsely chopped	1/3 c. olive oil
1/2 c. minced fresh parsley	1/4 c. drained capers
	1 T. fresh lemon juice

Combine all ingredients in food processor. Process, using on and off turns until well blended. Place in medium bowl and season to taste with salt and pepper. (May be made a day ahead of time.) Serve as a dip for vegetables, a spread for toasted pita triangles or as a spread for sandwiches.

EGGPLANT CAPONATA

Lorraine Mondulick

1 med. eggplant, peeled	1 T. oregano
Olive oil	10 stuffed green olives, sliced
2 medium-sized onions, sliced	1 T. sugar
3 ribs celery, parboiled	1 T. wine vinegar
1 lg. can tomatoes	

In a large frying pan, brown eggplant in olive oil, remove from pan. Add onions and celery and more oil (if necessary) to pan. Cook until lightly browned. Add tomatoes, oregano, olives, sugar and vinegar. Cook 10 minutes. Return eggplant and cook 10 more minutes. Adjust seasoning to taste. After cooling in refrigerator, serve as an antipasto. May be used as a side dish for grilled meats, chicken or fish. Allow two to three days to make before serving.

GUACAMOLE

Michelle James

Finely chopped garlic
Finely chopped onion
Chopped cilantro
Several dashes hot sauce

Med. salsa
1 can chopped tomatoes (opt.)
Salt & pepper (opt.)

Combine all ingredients to taste.

HOT CHEDDAR BEAN DIP

Barbara Limon

1 can bean & bacon soup (DO
  NOT DILUTE)
1 c. sour cream

1 T. dried minced onion
Dash of cayenne pepper
1½ c. grated cheddar cheese

Mix soup, sour cream, dried onion and pepper in a shallow baking dish. Top with cheese. Bake at 350° for 20 minutes. Serve with nacho blue chips.

FRENCH COUNTRY PATÉ

Lyn Griffiths

1 lb. sausage meat
2 lbs. ground chicken
1 T. brandy
2 bay leaves, chopped
2 sprigs fresh parsley

2 T. fresh chives
1 sprig fresh thyme
Salt & pepper
Bacon strips

Combine all ingredients except bacon. Line loaf pan with bacon strips. Fill terrine with mixture, cover with foil, place in bain marie. Cook at 350° for 1½ hours. Serve cold with buttered brown cocktail bread and gherkins.

NORWEGIAN PASTE

June Jorgensen

1 lb. cream cheese
1 tsp. salt
2 T. lemon or lime juice
½ tsp. ground black pepper
4 tins boneless/skinless
  sardines

2 T. chopped parsley
¼ tsp. Tabasco
Capers

Cream 1 pound cream cheese with 1 teaspoon salt, 2 tablespoons lemon or lime juice and ½ teaspoon freshly ground black pepper. Mash and beat in 4 tins boneless and skinless sardines, drained of most of

(continued)

12

34808-00

their oil, 2 tablespoons chopped parsley and ¼ teaspoon Tabasco. Taste for seasoning; add additional lemon juice, if desired. Form into a mound and garnish with capers and chopped parsley. Serve with toast fingers of thinly sliced bread.

SALMON PATE

June Jorgensen

1 lb. canned salmon
1 (8-oz.) pkg. cream cheese
2 T. grated onion
Pinch salt
1 T. lemon juice

1 T. horseradish
Pepper
Parsley sprigs
Paprika

Drain salmon and remove skin and bones. Flake and combine with next 6 ingredients. Refrigerate for 3 hours. Decorate with parsley and paprika; serve with crackers or petite pumpernickel bread.

FROSTED PATE

June Jorgenson

1 lb. liverwurst
1 clove garlic, crushed

½ tsp. crushed basil leaves
3 T. minced onion

Cream Cheese Topping: Soften 1 (8-ounce) package cream cheese, mix with 1 teaspoon mayonnaise, 1 clove garlic, crushed with dash of Tabasco. Mash liverwurst with fork. Mix in garlic, basil and onion thoroughly. Place on serving plate, shape mixture into loaf with rounded top. Chill. Spread cream cheese topping over loaf. Cover and refrigerate overnight. Before serving, ring caviar or sliced olives around topping. Garnish with parsley.

CHICKPEA, OLIVE AND ROASTED RED PEPPER PATE

Andrea Junghans

1 can chickpeas, roughly
  chopped
1 jar green olives, roughly
  chopped

1 jar roasted red peppers,
  roughly chopped
1 clove minced garlic
½-¾ c. olive oil

In food processor rough chop chickpeas; empty into bowl. Roughly chop olives; add to chickpeas. Fine chop peppers; add to bowl. Add minced garlic and olive oil; mix well. Serve with cracker, French bread or bread sticks.

OLIVE AND GARLIC SPREAD

Jo Anne Dain

1 c. black olives, pitted
1 c. green olives with pimentos
2-3 garlic cloves, finely chopped
2 T. olive oil
¼ tsp. freshly ground black pepper

Place olives, garlic, olive oil and black pepper in food processor and mix until roughly chopped. Serve with crackers or sourdough bread.

HOT SAUCE SALSA

Carmen Raddatz

1 lb. whole peeled tomatoes
3 jalapeño peppers, sliced
1 tsp. basil
½ tsp. baking soda
1 onion, quartered
Pinch of salt
1 bag tortilla chips*

Throw all ingredients into a blender and mix at low speed. Pour into serving bowl. The longer it sets, the hotter it gets. Refrigerate unused portion. *Serve with tortilla chips.

JULIE'S SALSA

Julie Aranibar

12-16 plum tomatoes
1 bunch cilantro
Sm. bunch of celery leaves
1 sm. yellow or Spanish onion
1 lemon
1-2 chili peppers

Zest lemon, then slice and squeeze juice. Place celery leaves, cilantro and lemon zest and juice in food processor; pulse to fine chop. Add onion and chili pepper. Add tomatoes and pulse to desired consistency.

SALSA-STYLE BEAN DIP

Janet Schenone

2 (16-oz.) cans black-eyed peas
1 (16-oz.) can hominy
1 (16-oz.) can fresh cut
  tomatoes
1 sm. bottle Zesty Italian salad
  dressing
3-4 cloves chopped garlic
2 sm.-med. chopped jalapeño
  peppers
1 sm. red onion, chopped
1 sm. bunch scallions, chopped
Chopped fresh parsley

Mix garlic, jalapeños, parsley, onion and scallions and set aside. Combine peas, hominy, tomatoes and dressing in large bowl. Mix well. Add chopped ingredients. Serve with Fritos Scoops or tortilla chips. Best when refrigerated overnight.

34808-00

SPINACH BALLS

Lorraine Mondulick

2 boxes chopped spinach,
  thawed & drained
2 c. stuffing mix
2 lg. onions, chopped fine
5 lg. eggs, beaten
¾ c. melted butter

½ c. Parmesan cheese
12-oz. pkg. pork sausage,
  cooked & drained
1 T. garlic salt
½ tsp. thyme
½ tsp. black pepper

Mix ingredients. Form into small balls. Bake 20 minutes in a 350° oven. May be frozen. Thaw 20 minutes before cooking. Yield: 90.

SCOTTISH EGGS

Rita LeMieux

6 hard-boiled eggs
2 lbs. fresh sausage
1 c. grated onion

2 eggs, well beaten
1½ c. finely crushed corn flake
  crumbs

Shell eggs and refrigerate until cool. Mix together: sausage, onion, corn flake crumbs and one beaten egg. Divide mixture into six equal parts and flatten each portion into a patty. Place a hard-boiled egg in the center on each patty and fold around egg. Dip covered eggs in beaten egg and roll in corn flake crumbs. Chill one hour. Bake on baking pan at 350° for 45 to 60 minutes or until brown and crusty. Slice in half when room temperature. Serve hot or cold with spicy or hot mustard.

TAFFY APPLE DIP

Carmen Raddatz

1 (8-oz.) pkg. cream cheese,
  softened
¾ c. brown sugar
¼ c. powdered sugar

2 T. vanilla
1 c. chopped nuts
Apple wedges dipped in lemon
  juice

Mix softened cream cheese, brown sugar, powdered sugar and vanilla in a medium bowl using a hand mixer. Add chopped nuts. Place in serving bowl and surround with apple wedges.

FROZEN MARGARITAS

Lydia J. Kolbas

¾ c. tequila
¼ c. triple sec
1 (6-oz.) can frozen limeade

1 (6 oz.) sweet & sour mix
1 (6 oz.) club soda

Add all ingredients in blender. Fill with ice and blend. Salt margarita glasses. Pour blended mix.

PINEAPPLE RASPBERRY PUNCH

Roberta Barbaro

1 (46-oz.) can pineapple juice
4 c. light raspberry juice
1 pt. fresh or frozen raspberries

1 lemon, thinly sliced
Ice
Mint sprigs for garnish

Chill ingredients. Combine in punch bowl. Garnish with mint sprigs. Makes 13 (6-ounce) servings.

PARTY PUNCH

Helen Cueto

½ gal. ginger ale
½ qt. vodka
1 can chunk pineapple with juice
1 jar maraschino cherries with ½ their juice

1 lg. ctn. frozen orange juice, undiluted
1 lg. ctn. lemonade concentrate, undiluted
1 pkg. frozen strawberries

Mix all ingredients. Pour over ice.

MINT JULEP'S

Laura Mondulick

For The Syrup:

2¼ c. sugar
6 c. water
2 T. plus ½ T. fresh lime juice
1 (12-oz.) can frozen lemonade concentrate, thawed

Fresh mint sprigs
8 glasses
1½ T. crème de menthe syrup

Combine sugar, water in a saucepan. Stir until sugar is dissolved. Stir in lime juice, lemonade concentrate and heat to just below boiling point. Do not let mixture boil. Remove from heat and chill to form a thick syrup. Add 10 ounces of chilled water into a glass of crushed ice and garnish with sprig of fresh mint.

BAILEY'S IRISH CREAM

Leslie McQueen

1½ c. half & half
1 c. sweetened condensed milk
1 c. V.O.
1 capful coconut extract

1 capful almond extract
1 T. Hershey's syrup
3 eggs

Put all ingredients in blender and blend thoroughly. Refrigerate and/or pour over ice.

16

HOT CHOCOLATE MIX

Debbie Becker

1 (1-lb. 9-oz.) box milk
1 (11-oz.) jar Coffee-Mate
1 (1½-lb.) box Nestle Quik

1¾ c. granulated sugar or 1 box powdered sugar

Mix **all** ingredients together (i.e. powdered milk, Coffee-Mate, Nestle Quik and which sugar you prefer). Put in jar with fitted lid. For one cup of hot chocolate. Add 3 to 5 heaping teaspoons to hot water. Very thick and creamy.

Recipe Favorites

Recipe Favorites

34808-00

Soups, Salads & Vegetables

Helpful Hints

- Fresh lemon juice will remove onion scent from hands.

- To save money, pour all leftover vegetables and water in which they are cooked into a freezer container. When full, add tomato juice and seasoning to create a "free" soup.

- Three large stalks of celery, chopped and added to about two cups of beans (navy, brown, pinto, etc.), will make them easier to digest.

- When cooking vegetables that grow above ground, the rule of thumb is to boil them without a cover.

- A lump of sugar added to water when cooking greens helps vegetables retain their fresh color.

- Never soak vegetables after slicing; they will lose much of their nutritional value.

- Fresh vegetables require little seasoning or cooking. If the vegetable is old, dress it up with sauces or seasoning.

- To quickly bake potatoes, place them in boiling water for 10 to 15 minutes. Pierce their skins with a fork and bake in a preheated oven.

- To cut down on odors when cooking cabbage, cauliflower, etc..., add a little vinegar to the cooking water.

- To avoid tears when cutting onions, try cutting them under cold running water or briefly placing them in the freezer before cutting.

- A little vinegar or lemon juice added to potatoes before draining will make them extra white when mashed.

- To avoid toughened beans or corn, add salt midway through cooking.

- For an easy no-mess side dish, try grilling your vegetables along with your meat.

- To dress up buttered, cooked vegetables, sprinkle them with toasted sesame seeds, toasted chopped nuts, canned french-fried onions or slightly crushed seasoned croutons.

Soups, Salads & Vegetables

VICHYSSOISE

Lyn Griffiths

2 T. butter
3 med. onions, sliced
4 leeks, white part only, sliced
1 lg. garlic clove, minced
4 med. potatoes, sliced

1 qt. chicken broth
1 c. milk
1 c. cream (light)
Salt & white pepper
Fresh chives, minced

Melt butter, add onions, leeks and garlic. Sauté until yellow but not brown. Add potatoes and chicken broth. Simmer until potatoes are very soft. Add milk and cream; heat, but do not boil. Purée in small batches in food processor. Add salt and pepper to taste. Chill thoroughly. Thin with milk if too thick. Sprinkle with chives. Serve cold. Serves six.

CARROT VICHYSSOISE

Michelle James

2 lg. carrots, peeled & cut in pieces
2 med. potatoes, peeled & cubed
1 leek (white part only cut in pieces)

3 c. chicken broth
1 o. heavy cream
Salt & pepper
Chopped chives

Place carrots, potatoes and leeks in cuisinart, pulsate with metal blade until coarsely chopped. In large saucepan, combine vegetables and chicken broth; simmer for 30 minutes. Strain vegetables and save liquid. Purée vegetables completely. Add liquid, stir in cream. Season with salt and pepper. Garnish with chives.

DON'S GAZPACHO SOUP

Susan Moore

1 c. chopped, peeled tomato
½ c. chopped green pepper
½ c. chopped celery
½ c. chopped cucumber
¼ c. chopped onion
2 tsp. snipped parsley
1 tsp. snipped chives
1 sm. clove garlic, minced

2-3 T. tarragon wine vinegar
3 T. olive oil
1 tsp. salt
¼ tsp. pepper
½ tsp. Worcestershire sauce
2 c. tomato juice (can add more if you desire)

(continued)

Combine all ingredients in a stainless steel or glass bowl. Cover and chill at least 4 hours. Serve in chilled cups. Makes 6 servings.

Note: Feel free to vary quantity of chopped vegetables according to taste and availability.

COLD CUCUMBER SOUP

Pauline H. Vachon

1 lb. chopped cucumbers, peeled & washed	1 tsp. wine vinegar
2 T. butter or margarine	$\frac{1}{2}$ tsp. fresh or dried dill weed
$\frac{1}{4}$ c. chopped green onions	Salt & pepper to taste
4 c. chicken broth	$\frac{1}{2}$ c. sour cream
	Green food coloring (opt.)

Chop cucumbers into $\frac{1}{2}$-inch chunks. Melt margarine in a large saucepan. Stir in onions and sauté for 2 minutes. Add cucumbers, chicken broth, vinegar and dill weed and bring to a boil. Reduce heat and simmer for 20 minutes. Remove from heat; let cool slightly. Purée mixture in a large blender or processor. Stir in sour cream and chill several hours. Just before serving, pour into bowls, top with a dollop of sour cream and additional chopped cucumbers for garnish.

Note: A few drops of food coloring may be added. Serves 8.

GINGER CARROT AND SWEET POTATO SOUP

Linda DeRogatis

1-lb. bag carrots, peeled & cubed	1 sm. onion, diced
2 lg. sweet potatoes, peeled & cubed	4 c. canned chicken broth
1 garlic clove, minced	1 c. evaporated skim milk
1 tsp. fresh ginger	$\frac{1}{4}$ tsp. salt
	$\frac{1}{4}$ tsp. pepper

In a stockpot, combine carrots, sweet potatoes, garlic, ginger, onion and stock. Bring to a boil. Turn heat down and simmer until carrots and potatoes are tender (about 35 minutes). Remove from heat and purée in a food processor or blender until smooth. Pour back into pot and add milk. Reheat slowly until hot. Serves 6.

34808-00

SIMPLE MINESTRONE SOUP

Lorraine Mondulick

1 lb. ground steak
2 T. olive oil
2 med. onions, sliced thin
⅛ tsp. marjoram
½ bay leaf
2 cans red kidney beans, juice
  included

1 can tomatoes
1 c. shredded cabbage
1 c. cooked macaroni
1 c. water
1 tsp. garlic salt
¼ tsp. pepper

Sauté ground round in olive oil, until it is broken up. Add onions, marjoram, bay leaf and sauté 5 minutes longer. Add beans and tomatoes to the meat mixture. Continue to cook over very low heat for 40 minutes, covered. Ten minutes before serving, add cabbage and cooked macaroni. Simmer 10 minutes. Add garlic salt and pepper. Let stand a few minutes before serving.

CAPTAIN THOM'S FISH CHOWDER

Marti Smith

3-4 filets fish (Sheephead is
  great) or snook, red fish or
  trout
1 sm.-med. onion to taste
4 lg. potatoes
Carrots (as many as you like)

Celery (handful)
Heavy whipping cream
Salt & pepper to taste
4 pieces bacon
½ stick butter

Parboil the fish in enough water to cover it. Add chopped onions and celery. Cook until fish is done or flaky. When done, remove fish and break up, if it is not already in small pieces. Salt and pepper is added to water while boiling. **Save water.** While the fish is cooking, peel potatoes and carrots and cut into bite-size pieces. Boil these until soft. (This can be done in the microwave.) It is good to take a little of the fish water to add flavor to the vegetables. Just put it with the water you are cooking the vegetables in. Cook bacon until crunchy. Put aside. In a large pot, mix together about 3 cups of the fish water, the same amount of heavy cream, cooked fish, cooked vegetables, crunched bacon, butter (to taste) and **very little** of the bacon grease. Add salt and pepper to taste. Let this **almost** come to a boil, then cook on low for awhile until flavors blend together.

CREAMY SEAFOOD CHOWDER

Jan Winn

2 T. butter, divided
½ lb. shrimp, peeled & deveined
½ lb. scallops
1 lb. crab (imitation may be
  used)
1 onion, chopped
2 ribs celery, sliced
2 lg. pieces white fish (cod)

1 T. thyme
1 red bell pepper, chopped
3 c. half & half
¼ c. sherry
½ tsp. salt
½ tsp. cayenne pepper
⅛ tsp. nutmeg

In large skillet, melt 1 tablespoon butter. Add shrimp and scallops; cook until opaque. Remove. In same pan melt remaining butter over medium heat. Add onion, celery and thyme, cook until tender, 10 minutes. Add bell pepper. Cook until crisp tender, 5 minutes. Add half & half, sherry, cayenne, nutmeg, salt, white fish, crab and 1 cup water. Bring to boil, turn heat down gently simmer to heat through.

CHEESY SEAFOOD CHOWDER

Ken Scott

¼ c. water
1 (7-oz.) pkg. Gouda cheese,
  shredded
1 (12-oz.) pkg. frozen cooked
  shrimp, thawed
½ c. dry white wine (opt.)
6 T. butter
¾ c. chopped celery
½ c. shredded carrot

½ c. chopped onion
½ c. flour
1 tsp. thyme, crushed
½ tsp. salt
¼ tsp. pepper
1 (14½-oz.) can chicken broth
1 (6-oz.) can tomato paste
4 c. milk
2 (6½-oz.) cans clams, drained

In heavy 4-quart saucepan, melt butter over medium heat. Add vegetables and cook until tender, about 8 minutes. Stir in flour and seasonings until smooth. Remove from heat. Stir in tomato paste. Gradually stir in milk, broth and water. Bring to a boil and cook for 1 minute over medium heat, stirring constantly. Reduce heat to low. Stir in cheese until melted (**do not boil**). Stir in clams and shrimp; heat through. Just before serving, stir in wine, if desired. Makes ten (1-cup) servings.

34808-00

MANHATTAN CLAM CHOWDER

Joe Cueto

2 (20-oz.) cans whole baby
  clams
½ c. finely diced bacon
1 med. onion, thinly sliced
1-2 c. diced raw potatoes
1 stalk celery, chopped
1 green pepper, chopped
1 tsp. salt
⅛ tsp. thyme

1 bay leaf
5 c. liquid (calm liquor plus
  water)
1 (20-oz.) can tomatoes
1 tsp. salt
½ tsp. caraway seeds
½ tsp. oregano
⅛ tsp. pepper

Drain clams and save liquor. Fry bacon until crisp. Add onion, celery
and pepper. Cook until tender. Add potatoes, bay leaf and liquid. Cover
and simmer 10 to 15 minutes until potatoes are tender. Chop clams,
add tomatoes, clams and seasonings, bring to a simmer do not boil.

BROCCOLI CHEDDAR CHEESE SOUP

Laura Mondulick

¼ c. butter or margarine
1½ c. chopped onion
1 c. chopped celery
2 pkgs. frozen chopped broccoli
3 (10¾-oz.) cans chicken broth

8 oz. sharp cheddar cheese,
  shredded
½ c. half-and-half
¼ tsp. nutmeg
Salt & pepper to taste

Defrost broccoli. In 2-quart casserole, combine margarine, onions and
celery. Cover. Microwave on high 10 minutes, stirring once or twice.
Add drained broccoli to the mixture. Purée 2 cups at a time in blender.
Pour into 2-quart measuring cup. Add boiling chicken broth, half-and-
half and nutmeg to the mixture. Microwave on high 8 minutes or until
nearly boiling. Stir in cheese. Add salt and pepper to taste. Let stand
5 minutes. Makes 8 (1-cup) servings.

TOMATO FLORENTINE SOUP

Fran Moorehead

2 T. butter or margarine
1 lg. onion, chopped
1½ c. tomato juice
2 pkts. vegetable broth mix
1 c. water
6 lg. tomatoes, peeled, seeded &
  chopped

½ tsp. celery seed
½ tsp. celery salt
½ tsp. pepper
1 c. spinach leaves, chopped

Sauté onion in butter. Add to tomato juice, water and seasonings in
3-quart pot. Simmer slowly while preparing tomatoes. Add tomatoes

(continued)

and cook for 15 minutes. Add chopped spinach. Turn off heat, cover and let set for 15 minutes before serving.

FRESH CREAM OF TOMATO SOUP

Suzanne Kindor

12-14 ripe tomatoes	4 T. butter or margarine
2 T. salt	4 T. flour
1 T. sugar	1½ c. milk or cream

Quarter and stew tomatoes. (No need to peel, just quarter.) Drain off excess liquid (save). Put stewed tomatoes through a food mill. Add salt and sugar or to taste) to pulp. Make a white sauce with butter, flour and milk. Gradually pour warm pulp into sauce. If necessary thin with saved stewing liquid.

CHOW-DOWN CHOWDER

Debbie Becker

1 (20-oz.) pkg. refrigerated shredded potatoes	2 c. skim milk
	¼ tsp. pepper
1 (14½-oz.) reduced-sodium chicken broth	⅓ c. sliced green onions
	12 oz. 97% fat free link sausage,
1 (10-oz.) pkg. frozen whole kernel corn	sliced (Hillshire Farms is good)

In a 4-quart Dutch oven, combine shredded potatoes, chicken broth and corn. Bring mixture just to boiling; reduce heat. Simmer covered for 10 minutes or until potatoes are just tender. Using a potato masher, slightly mash potatoes. Stir in 2 cups milk. Then in separate skillet, cook sausage until done. Then add sausage, green onions and pepper to chowder in Dutch oven. Season to taste with salt and pepper, cilantro and red bottled hot pepper sauce.

CHICKEN-AVOCADO TORTILLA SOUP

Debbie Becker

⅓ c. chopped onion	1 (14-oz.) can diced tomatoes
3 cloves garlic, chopped	1 (4-oz.) can diced green chilies
¾ tsp. ground cumin	10 (6-inch) corn tortillas
¾ tsp. oregano	1½ lbs. boned, skinned chicken
¼ tsp. chili powder	breasts
¼ tsp. pepper	1 firm ripe avocado
2 T. cilantro	½ c. shredded sharp cheddar
8 c. chicken broth	cheese

In a 5 to 6-quart saucepan, stir onion, garlic, cumin, oregano, chili powder and pepper until spices are fragrant (about 1 minute). Add broth,

(continued)

34808-00

tomatoes (including juice) and green chilies. Cover and bring to a boil. Stack tortillas and cut into ⅛-inch wide strips. Add to boiling broth. Reduce heat, cover and simmer for 15 minutes, stirring occasionally. Rinse chicken and cut into ½-inch pieces. Peel the avocado, pit and thinly slice. Add chicken to broth and return to a boil over high heat. Reduce heat, cover and simmer until chicken is white in center (test), about 5 minutes. Stir in cilantro and salt to taste. Ladle into soup bowls, garnish with avocado and add cheese to taste. Prep and cook time: about 30 minutes.

SOUTHWESTERN BEAN SOUP

Angela Smith

3 diced onions
3 diced (red & green) peppers
2 cans corn
1 can black beans
1 can red beans
1 can navy beans
5 c. chicken stock
Season to taste with: cumino, chili powder & salt

Sauté onion, place onion, pepper, corn, black beans, red beans, navy beans and chicken stock in stockpot. Season with cumin, chili powder and salt to taste. Bring to boil, then simmer for 1 hour.

REL'S CHILI SOUP

Roberta Barbaro

1 (3-oz.) can chopped green chili peppers (use only ¾ of can)
2 cans cream of mushroom soup
1 c. sour cream
1½ c. half & half or milk

Blend chili peppers and soup. Add sour cream and half & half. Blend and heat.

NEW ORLEANS CHICKEN GUMBO

Kathy Tudyk

2 qt. chicken stock
1½ c. fresh tomatoes, chopped
1 c. fresh okra
1½ c. finely diced, cooked chicken
¼ c. green onion, finely cut
½ c. green pepper, finely cut
2½ c. cooked rice
1 c. finely cut celery
½ c. butter
¼ c. chicken fat (I use butter)
½ c. flour

Sauté onions and celery 5 minutes in butter. Add green peppers, cook 4 minutes. Add tomatoes, cook 8 minutes. Make a roux by cooking together for 4 minutes ¼ cup chicken fat or butter and ½ cup flour;

(continued)

add roux to hot chicken stock slowly to avoid lumps. Add onion etc. mixture along with okra, rice and chicken. Cook 10 more minutes. Serves 12 to 14.

RAVIOLI SOUP

Jane Goodrich

¾ lb. Italian sausage
1 (14½-oz.) can Del Monte fresh cut diced tomatoes with basil, garlic & oregano
1 (14-oz.) can beef broth

1 (9-oz.) pkg. fresh or frozen cheese ravioli or tortellini
1 (14½-oz.) can green beans, drained
2 onions, sliced

In 5-quart pot, cook meat; drain. Add tomatoes, broth and 1¾ cups water, bring to a boil. Reduce heat; stir in ravioli and cook according to directions. Add beans and onions; heat through. Season with pepper and sprinkle with grated Parmesan cheese.

HUNGARIAN GULYAS SOUP

Julia Borsos

2½ c. cubed beef
4 T. or 1 c. oil
1 c. onion
2 T. paprika
Salt
Garlic

Caraway seeds
Soup pasta
1¾ lbs. potatoes
1 c. green pepper
1 sm. fresh tomato
1 c. carrot

Cube the beef into ¾-inch pieces. Fry chopped onion in the melted shortening until it is golden yellow. Lower heat, add paprika, stir rapidly. Add meat, keep stirring, add salt. When the meat is browned and all the liquid is evaporated, add the caraway seeds, finely chopped garlic and a small amount of cold water, cover and braise the meat slowly. Stir in occasionally and add small quantities of water, if necessary. The meat should be braised, not boiled. While the meat is cooking, cube the potatoes, carrots, green pepper and tomato into pieces, ⅓ inch size. Just before the meat is completely tender, add the cubed potatoes, brown slightly. Add stock, green pepper, carrots and tomato. When the potato is almost cooked and the soup is ready to served, add the pasta and adjust the quantity of stock or water.

34808-00

FRUIT SALAD

Jane Goodrich

2 T. butter
4 T. sugar
2 tsp. lemon juice
2 egg yolks
2 apples, cut

2 oranges, cut
2 bananas, cut
½ c. grapes
Sm. can pineapple chunks
½ pt. whipping cream

Combine butter, sugar and lemon juice. Beat good and cook until light colored and thick. Cool; beat egg whites, mix with above. Add ½ pint whipping cream, whipped. Cut up 2 apples, 2 oranges, 2 bananas, ½ cup grapes and small can cubed pineapple. Mix with sauce, chill several hours.

CENTRAL VALLEY SALAD

Lyn Griffiths

1 lg. head romaine
¼ lb. red/black grapes, halved
2 sm. oranges, peeled,
  sectioned

1 sm. red onion, sliced
1 avocado, sliced

Lemon Mustard Dressing:

1 c. olive oil
¼ c. lemon juice
½ tsp. salt
1 tsp. Worcestershire sauce

1½ tsp. Dijon mustard
1½ tsp. honey
¼ tsp. white pepper

Combine all ingredients. Shake vigorously until well blended. Makes 1½ cups. Tear lettuce, toss with red/black grapes, oranges, onion and avocado. Just before serving, toss with Lemon Mustard dressing. Serves six.

MANDARIN ORANGE SALAD

Jan Winn

1 (16-oz.) can mandarin oranges
5 c. romaine lettuce
½ c. slivered almonds, toasted
2 T. sliced green onions
3 T. honey

3 T. mandarin orange juice
3 T. vinegar
½ tsp. prepared mustard
1 tsp. vegetable oil
2 tsp. water

Drain mandarin orange and reserve juice. Combine oranges, lettuce, almonds and green onions in large bowl, toss gently. Combine honey, juice, vinegar, mustard, oil and water. Pour over salad, mix and serve.

TURTLE BEACH SALAD

Sonya Smetzer

Chill ingredients before
  assembling; drain cans and
  combine:

2 (16-oz.) cans cut green beans
  (OR 1 lb. fresh steamed green
  beans)

2 sm. cans mandarin oranges
1 sm. can diced water chestnuts

Add:

2 branches chopped celery
½ c. pecans or walnuts

¼ c. raspberry-walnut
  vinaigrette dressing (Ken's)

Toss lightly and serve at once.

ORANGE, AVOCADO, ALMOND SALAD

Andrea Junghans

1 head romaine lettuce
2 avocados, sliced
3 navel oranges (segments)

1 bunch fresh cilantro, chopped
1½ c. almond (stick or slivers)
1 bunch spring onions, chopped

Wash and tear romaine into bite-size pieces, slice peeled avocados, peel and segment oranges, wash and chop cilantro, wash and chop spring onions. Toss together with almonds. Use either bottled Italian dressing or favorite vinaigrette. **For thicker dressing:** Purée bottle of dressing with ½ orange and ½ avocado. Great with grilled salmon on the side or tossed together! Serves 6 to 8.

CHINESE SALAD

Claire Akey

1 head Napa cabbage, crisped
1-2 bunches scallions, sliced
2 pkgs. ramen noodle soup
  (break pkt. & discard
  seasoning before opening)

1 (8-oz.) pkg. sliced almonds
Sesame seeds

Dressing:

¾ c. oil
¼ c. cider vinegar

½ c. sugar
2 T. soy sauce

Combine in small skillet, oil, vinegar, sugar and soy sauce. Do not stir. Cool and refrigerate. Pour over tossed salad.

34808-00

COUSCOUS SALAD WITH CUCUMBER, PEPPERS AND TOMATOES

Michelle Winter

1 c. water
1 c. couscous
¼ tsp. salt
Salt to taste
2 green bell peppers
½ lb. cherry tomatoes, halved
1 cucumber, peeled, seeded & diced into ½-inch cubes
3 cloves minced garlic

1 sm. green or red jalapeño or serrano chili, seeded & minced
½ c. chopped fresh cilantro
6 T. extra virgin olive oil
5 T. fresh lemon juice
1½ tsp. ground cumin
½ tsp. paprika
Freshly ground pepper

Preheat boiler. In a saucepan, boil water. Add couscous and ½ teaspoon salt. Stir well, cover and let stand 10 minutes. Uncover and transfer to a large shallow baking dish, fluffing with a fork and spreading evenly. Let cool completely. Cut bell peppers in half; remove seeds and ribs. Place on baking sheet, cut sides down and broil until skins blacken and blister. Remove peppers from broiler and drape loosely with aluminum foil for 10 minutes until cool. Using small knife, remove skins. Cut peppers into ½-inch square. Transfer couscous into large bowl. Scatter bell peppers, tomatoes, cucumbers, chili pepper and cilantro over top. In a small bowl, whisk together olive oil, lemon juice, cumin, paprika and garlic. Season with salt and pepper to taste. Add to couscous and toss together well. Adjust seasoning to taste before serving, if necessary.

AVOCADO SALAD WITH HONEY DRESSING

Leslie McQueen

1 pkg. lemon Jello
1 c. boiling water
1 c. sour cream
1 c. mayonnaise

Juice of 1 fresh lemon
Dash of Tabasco
2 avocados, mashed

Dissolve Jello in water. Add other ingredients. Pour into mold and chill until firm. Unmold and surround with fresh fruit. Serve with honey dressing. Serves 6.

JELLO MOLD

Leslie McQueen

1 sm. pkg. lime Jello
½ chopped apple, diced with skin (red apple)

½ c. chopped celery, diced
½ c. mayonnaise
½ c. chopped walnuts

Dissolve Jello according to package directions. Put a little into mold. Just straight Jello! Refrigerate for ½ hour at most. In the meantime,

(continued)

29

mix and whip the mayonnaise into remaining Jello with an electric mixer. Fold in all ingredients with a spoon. Pour on top. Stir once or twice so that fruit doesn't bunch up. Refrigerate. When ready, invert on plate.

LULU'S SET SALAD

Gerry Haller

1 pkg. lemon or lime Jello
1 c. hot water
1 pkg. Philadelphia cream
 cheese

½ c. cut-up celery (sm.)
1 sm. can crushed pineapple
½ pt. whipping cream
Nuts, if desired

Dissolve cheese in Jello. When **cool** add to **whipped** cream. Add other ingredients. Do not drain pineapple juice, use the whole can. Pour into a "ring" container and refrigerate until set.

BLUEBERRY SALAD

Pauline Bridge

1 (6-oz.) pkg. raspberry Jello
1 pkg. Knox gelatin, softened in
 ¼ c. water
2 c. hot water
1 (20-oz.) can crushed
 pineapple, undrained

1 (21-oz.) can blueberry pie
 filling
½ c. pecans toasted in 1 T.
 butter

Topping:

8 oz. Philadelphia cream cheese
1 c. sour cream
½ c. sugar

1 tsp. vanilla
Some powdered sugar to firm

Add hot water to Jello, add softened gelatin and fruits. Refrigerate until solid. In 13 x 9 x 2-inch pan soften cream cheese. Add sour cream, sugar and vanilla and some powdered sugar. Cover Jello. Toast pecans in butter for 5 to 10 minutes at 350°. Sprinkle over topping. Chill.

CRANBERRY SALAD

Carmen Raddatz

1 lb. raw cranberries
2 c. sugar
1 med. can crushed pineapples

1 lg. bag miniature
 marshmallows
1 lg. Cool Whip

Use blender **or** food processor to grind cranberries. Combine cranberries and sugar in large bowl; let stand 1 to 2 hours. Add pineapple and marshmallows let set 1 hour until marshmallows soak up juice. Add ¾ of Cool Whip and mix well. Can refrigerate or freeze. Add balance of Cool Whip a garnish before serving.

34808-00

CRAN-RASPBERRY SALAD

Dolores Whittum

1 pkg. raspberry gelatin
1 pkg. lemon gelatin
1½ c. boiling water
1 (10-oz.) pkg. frozen
  raspberries

1 (16-oz.) can jellied cranberry
  sauce
1 (7-oz.) bottle lemon-lime
  carbonated beverage or ginger
  ale

Dissolve 2 gelatins in boiling water; stir in frozen raspberries, breaking into large pieces. Add cranberry sauce and break up with a fork. Slowly add carbonated beverage. Turn into 6-cup mold. Chill 5 to 6 hours or overnight.

TAFFY APPLE SALAD

Shirley Grube

1 lg. can chunk pineapple
  (drained & save juice)
2 c. sm. marshmallows
½ c. sugar
1 T. flour

1 egg, well beaten
1½ T. white vinegar
1 (12 oz.) Cool Whip
2 c. unpeeled diced apples
1½ c. cocktail peanuts

(A.) Mix pineapple chunks and marshmallows, refrigerate overnight. (B.) Mix juice, flour, sugar, vinegar and egg; cook until thick. Refrigerate overnight. Mix Cool Whip with A and B. Then add apples and peanuts and mix well.

CURRIED APPLE, CHICKEN SALAD

Andrea Junghans

3 c. cooked, cubed chicken
  breasts
1 c. Hellmann's mayonnaise
1 c. sour cream
2 T. curry powder
3 Red Delicious apples cored &
  cubed

1 c. seedless grapes
1 bunch cilantro
3 spring onions
Salt to taste

Combine chicken, cubed apples, seedless grapes, chopped cilantro and chopped spring onions. Mix curry, mayonnaise and sour cream until well blended. Toss with everything. Serve cold with mini croissants. Serves 6 to 8.

3-BEAN SALAD

Mary Button
Darlene Jenny

1 (16-oz.) can cut green beans
1 (16-oz.) can cut yellow wax
  beans
1 (16-oz.) can red kidney beans
¼ c. green pepper
1 med. onion

½ c. cider vinegar
⅓ c. salad oil
1 c. sugar
1 tsp. salt
1 tsp. pepper

Rinse beans and drain well. Chop green pepper. Thinly slice onion. Combine beans, green pepper and onion. Combine remaining ingredients. Add to bean mixture. Toss well and chill overnight.

HOT CHICKEN SALAD

June Jorgensen

4 lg. chicken breasts, cooked &
  cut in pieces
2 c. celery, diced
¾ c. diced almonds
1¼ tsp. salt
2 T. lemon juice

1¼ c. mayonnaise
¼ lb. sharp cheddar cheese (1
  c. grated)
1 lg. can sliced mushrooms
Potato chips

Mix all ingredients and place in a buttered 2-quart casserole. Crumble potato chips, coarsely crushed, on top. Bake in a 350° oven about 20 minutes.

HOT SPINACH SALAD

Linda Kammerer

8 oz. fresh cleaned spinach
½ red onion, julienned
4 oz. sliced mushrooms
½ lb. bacon, diced
2 oz. red wine vinegar
2 oz. olive oil

2 oz. sour cream
2 oz. honey
½ T. poppy seeds
1 T. black pepper
½ tsp. salt

Sauté bacon until crisp. Drain. Add red onions and mushrooms and sauté until onions become transparent. Add remaining ingredients and heat. Add spinach and toss lightly. Serve immediately. Serves 8.

34808-00

FRENCH ONION CASSEROLE

Helen Cueto

3 lg. sweet onions
2 T. butter or margarine
1 (8-oz.) pkg. fresh mushrooms, sliced
2 c. (8 oz.) shredded Swiss cheese, divided
1 (10¾-oz.) can condensed cream of mushroom soup

1 (5-oz.) can evaporated milk
2 tsp. soy sauce
6 (½-inch thick) slices French bread
¼ c. finely chopped fresh parsley

Slice onions crosswise. Melt butter in large skillet. Cook onions and mushrooms, stirring until tender. Spoon mixture into a lightly greased 2-quart baking dish. Sprinkle with 1 cup cheese. Combine soup, milk and soy sauce; pour over cheese. Top with bread slices and sprinkle with remaining 1 cup cheese and parsley. Cover and refrigerate 4 to 8 hours. Remove baking dish from refrigerator and let stand at room temperature 30 minutes. Bake covered at 375° for 30 minutes. Bake covered at 375° for 30 minutes. Uncover and bake 15 to 20 minutes or until thoroughly heated.

DAWN'S CHEESY BAKED ONIONS

Susan Moore

2 med. sweet onions
3 T. butter or margarine
2 T. flour

¼ tsp. salt
1 c. milk
⅔ c. shredded cheddar cheese

Slice onion and separate into rings. Grease bottom and sides of a 1-quart baking dish. Place onions in baking dish in layers. Set aside. Melt butter in a small saucepan over very low heat. Slowly add flour and salt, stirring until smooth. Gradually add milk, stirring constantly. Bring to a boil, then immediately reduce heat to low and stir for about two minutes, until sauce is smooth and creamy. Remove pot from heat and stir in cheese. Pour sauce over onions and bake uncovered at 350° for 45 to 50 minutes until onions are tender and cheese is a bit browned. Serves 4.

GRILLED VEGETABLES WITH BALSAMIC VINAIGRETTE

Janet Barry

1 med. eggplant
2 med. zucchini
2-3 med. yellow squash
2 med. red bell pepper
¾ c. olive oil
¼ c. balsamic vinegar

1 tsp. salt
¼ tsp. black pepper
1 clove garlic, minced
2-3 T. finely chopped
Mixed fresh herbs

(continued)

Trim, then slice eggplant, zucchini and yellow squash lengthwise into ¼ to ½-inch thick slices. Core, seed and cut red pepper into 1-inch wide strips. Place vegetables in a deep serving platter. In a small bowl combine remaining ingredients. Pour vinaigrette over vegetables; turn to coat. Let stand 30 minutes or longer. Remove vegetables to grill. Reserve platter with remaining vinaigrette. Oil grid to prevent sticking. Grill vegetables on a covered grill, over medium heat 8 to 16 minutes until fork-tender, turning once or twice. As vegetables are done, return them to the platter, then turn to coat with vinaigrette. Serve warm. Makes 6 servings.

ASPARAGUS VINAIGRETTE

Jane Stanton

1 lb. thin asparagus
¾ c. olive oil
¼ c. lemon juice
Salt to taste
½ tsp. dry mustard
Freshly ground pepper to taste

1 T. chopped capers
1 tsp. finely chopped pickle
½ tsp. finely chopped parsley
½ tsp. finely chopped chervil
½ tsp. finely chopped chives

Steam the asparagus for 2 minutes. Drain and plunge into cold water. Drain. Combine olive oil, lemon juice, salt, dry mustard, pepper, capers, pickle, parsley, chervil and chives, mixing well. Pour over asparagus and chill from 2 to 5 hours. Garnish with thin slices of red pepper.

MY DAD'S GREEN BEANS

Linda Spahr

2 lbs. fresh green beans
½ lb. bacon
1 med. onion, diced
½ c. red wine vinegar

¼ c. sugar
Salt & pepper to taste
1½ c. water

Cut bacon into small pieces. Sauté bacon and onion in heavy pot. Add beans, sugar, vinegar, water, salt and pepper. Cover. Simmer about one hour or until beans are done.

POP CARROTS

Shirley Cote

1 lg. bag fresh carrots
1 stick butter

7-Up or soda water
Salt & pepper to taste

Melt butter in saucepan large enough to hold carrots; cut to bite-size pieces. Put carrots in saucepan and over with soda. Boil until liquid is gone. Add salt and pepper, if desired.

34

SNOW'S SCALLOPED TOMATOES

Ken Mondulick

1 lg. can Italian plum tomatoes
⅓ c. melted butter
2½ c. stale white bread, cubed
1 tsp. salt

3 T. brown sugar
Parmesan cheese
Thyme

Mix bread cubes and melted butter. Heat tomatoes, salt and brown sugar until slowly boiling. Pour over bread mixture. Pour into a greased baking dish. Sprinkle with cheese and thyme. Bake at 425° for 30 to 45 minutes.

CORN PUDDING

Shirley Grube

2 eggs
½ tsp. salt
Pinch of pepper
Pinch of onion salt

½ c. bread crumbs
2-3 T. milk
2 cans cream-style corn

Beat eggs in bowl. Add salt, pepper and onion salt. Add bread crumbs, milk and mix well. Add corn and pour into greased casserole. Sprinkle bread crumbs on top. (Do not cover.) Bake in 350° oven for 35 to 40 minutes until set and not too thin. Can be frozen for 1 week and reheated.

CORN PUDDING

Carol Leslie Feintuch

1 can corn
1 can cream-style corn
1 stick butter

1 box Jiffy corn muffin mix
1 c. sour cream

Blend corn, cream-style corn, butter, muffin mix and sour cream. Pour into casserole. Bake at 375° for 45 to 60 minutes until brown. Serve uncovered.

CORN SOUFFLÉ

Jane Stanton

16-oz. can cream-style corn
½ c. milk
2 T. cornstarch

1 T. sugar
3 eggs, beaten
Salt & pepper to taste

Combine cornstarch and milk. Mix until cornstarch is dissolved. In a large bowl combine corn, cornstarch, milk mixture, sugar, eggs and salt and pepper. With a wire whisk mix all ingredients. Place in a casserole. Bake uncovered in a preheated 350° oven for 1 hour.

SQUASH CASSEROLE

Mary Button
Darlene Jenny

6 c. sliced yellow squash
½ c. chopped onion
1 can cream of chicken soup
1 c. sour cream

½ c. margarine or butter
1 (8-oz.) pkg. herb stuffing mix
½ tsp. salt

Cook squash and onion until tender in boiling water with ½ teaspoon salt. Combine separately soup and sour cream. Fold in squash and onion. Combine separately margarine and stuffing mix. Spread ½ of stuffing mix in bottom of 9 x 12-inch greased baking dish. Spread vegetable mix on, then top with remaining stuffing mix. Bake at 350° for 25 to 30 minutes.

ZUCCHINI FRITTERS

Ellen Grabowski

1½ c. flour
1½ tsp. baking powder
¼ tsp. salt
⅔ c. milk
½ c. chopped onion

1 well-beaten egg
3 T. grated cheese
1 med. zucchini, grated
1 T. oil

Mix all ingredients well. Drop by tablespoon into hot oil until brown.

SIMPLE POTATO SALAD

Rhonda Maule

10 med. potatoes, peeled
⅓ c. chopped chives
¼ c. vegetable oil
¼ c. vinegar
Sm. onion, chopped fine

1½ tsp. salt
¼ tsp. pepper
¾ c. mayonnaise or to taste
½ c. celery, finely sliced
3 hard-boiled eggs, sliced

Boil potatoes until tender. Drain potatoes, cool. In large bowl combine chives, oil, vinegar, onion, salt and pepper; mix well. Cut potatoes into cubes; add oil mixture to coat. Cover, refrigerate at least 2 hours. Before serving, fold in mayonnaise, celery and eggs.

PARTY POTATOES

Leslie McQueen

¼ c. melted butter
1 can cream of mushroom soup
1 c. milk (mixed & preheated)
1 pt. sour cream

2 c. grated cheese (cheddar)
1 lg. pkg. frozen hash brown
  potatoes

(continued)

36

34808-00

Mix and stir well to coat. Spread into a 9 x 13-inch pan and bake for 1 hour at 350°. Spread two cans of onion rings over top for last 15 minutes.

NANA'S POTATOES

Debra Weber
S. Grube

½ lb. bacon, cooked & crumbled
2-lb. pkg. frozen hash brown potatoes

1-lb. pkg. Velveeta cheese
2 c. mayonnaise
½ c. chopped onion

Melt cheese in microwave, add mayonnaise and ¾ of bacon. Mix in potatoes. Top with rest of the bacon. Bake 40 minutes at 350°.

OLD FASHION POTATO PANCAKES

Carol Leslie Feintuch

4 lg. potatoes (1½ lbs.), peeled
1 med. onion
1 T. chopped parsley (opt.)
1 egg
1 tsp. salt
¼ tsp. pepper

2 T. all-purpose flour
½ tsp. baking powder
About ½ c. oil for frying (vegetable)
Applesauce or sour cream for serving

Grate potatoes and onion, in food processor. Transfer to a colander to drain out as much liquid as possible. In large bowl combine potatoes, onion, parsley, egg, salt, pepper, flour and baking powder; mix well. Heat oil in a heavy skillet. Drop 2 tablespoons of potato mixture into pan. Flatten with back of spoon. Fry each side until golden brown and crispy. Drain on paper towels. Serve hot with applesauce or sour cream.

NO-FRY POTATOES

Leslie McQueen

All natural Pam cooking spray
4 baking potatoes
Your favorite seasonings: such as salt and pepper, Cajun seasoning or garlic salt

Preheat oven to 400°. Spray a baking sheet with Pam. Cut each potato into 8 to 10 wedges. Arrange on baking sheet. Spray wedges with Pam for 5 seconds. Sprinkle with desired seasonings. Bake 30 to 40 minutes or until cooked through, turning potatoes every 15 minutes until crisp. Makes 4 to 6 servings.

AU GRATIN POTATOES

Shirley Cote

1 (2-lb.) pkg. frozen hash browns
1 can cream of celery soup
1 can cream of potato soup
1 (8-oz.) ctn. sour cream
1 lb. shredded cheddar cheese

Grease baking dish (13 x 9-inch) or casserole dish. Mix all ingredients together. Bake at 350° for 1 to 1½ hours.

POTATO PUDDING

Lyn Griffiths

3½ lbs. potatoes, peeled
1 lg. carrot, peeled
1 lg. onion, peeled
3 eggs
2 T. vegetable oil (canola)
1½ tsp. salt
½ tsp. pepper
¼ tsp. cinnamon

Heat oven to 400°. Grate by hand or shred in food processor potatoes, carrot and onion. Combine. Beat eggs until light and fluffy. Add eggs and remaining ingredients to potato mixture. Oil 1½-quart shallow pan. Pour mixture into prepared pan. Bake for 1 hour or until top of pudding is crisp and brown. Serves 8 to 10.

EASY POTATO CASSEROLE

Ellen Grabowski

3 cans sliced potatoes
1 can quartered artichoke in water
1 jar roasted red peppers (in oil)
1 sm. can sliced black olives
1 T. chopped garlic
1½ c. flavored bread crumbs
1 c. grated Parmesan cheese
Dash of oregano
1¼ c. vegetable oil

Mix all ingredients together. Let set in refrigerator 24 hours. Bake at 450° for 20 to 25 minutes or until hot and bubbly.

LINDA'S THANKSGIVING SWEET POTATOES

Linda Spahr

1 lg. (40-oz.) can sweet potatoes
1-2 T. sugar
½ tsp. cinnamon
½ tsp. nutmeg
4 T. melted butter

Topping:

¾ c. cornflakes, crushed
1 c. pecans
½ c. brown sugar
4-5 T. butter. melted

(continued)

34808-00

Mash sweet potatoes; stir in melted butter and sugar. Add cinnamon and nutmeg. Microwave until hot. While carving turkey, add topping and bake at 350° for 10 minutes. Serves 6.

SCALLOPED SWEET POTATOES AND APPLES

Marie Scott

6 medium-size sweet potatoes
½ c. brown sugar
4 T. butter

½ tsp. salt
1 tsp. mace
1½ c. sliced apples

Boil sweet potatoes until tender. Slice into ¼-inch sections. Butter baking dish (9 x 12 inches). Layer sweet potatoes on bottom, then apples. Sprinkle with sugar, salt and mace. Dot with butter. Repeat until dish is full, having apple layer on top. Bake in 350° oven for 50 minutes.

GREEN PEA PICNIC SALAD

Laura Mondulick

1 lb. frozen green peas
1 med. Kirby cucumber (¾ c. chopped)
2 cloves fresh garlic
¼ c. fresh basil leaves (opt.)
1 med. red bell pepper (1 c. chopped)

1 sm. onion
⅔ c. light sour cream
⅓ c. light mayonnaise
Juice from ½ a lemon (2 T.)
½ tsp. salt or more to taste
¼ tsp. pepper or more to taste

Place peas in a colander and run cool water over them to thaw. Set aside to drain well. Cut the cucumber in half and using a spoon, scrape out the seeds. Chop the cucumber and place it in a 2-quart or larger bowl. Peel and finely mince the garlic, adding it to the bowl. If using basil, chop the leaves and add them to the bowl, seed and chop the pepper, adding it to the bowl as you go. Peel and chop the onion, adding it to the bowl as you chop. Add the sour cream, mayonnaise, lemon, salt and pepper to the bowl. Stir well with the vegetables. Add the green peas, toss to coat and mix well. Serve at once or cover and chill up to 24 hours. Makes 5 cups.

COLD PASTA SALAD

Carol Leslie Feintuch

½ c. soy sauce
½ c. oil
2 tsp. garlic powder
Toasted sesame seeds
Dash Tabasco sauce

Dash Worcestershire sauce
1 box linguini
1 box frozen peas & carrots
1 sliced red pepper
1 bunch scallions, chopped

(continued)

34808-00

Mix soy sauce, oil, garlic powder, Tabasco and Worcestershire sauce. Shake and refrigerate for 1 hour. Break pasta in half. Cook and drain. Cook peas and carrots. Toss all together and refrigerate.

TANGY MACARONI SALAD

Donna Arakel

2 T. olive oil
1 lb. elbow macaroni
1 T. garlic powder
1 T. onion powder
1 T. meat tenderizer

1 c. mayonnaise
3 T. water
2 T. BBQ sauce (Masterpiece)
2 tsp. Worcestershire sauce
2 sm. tomatoes

Cook elbow macaroni "al dente". Cover macaroni with olive oil and mix. Add garlic powder, onion powder and meat tenderizer; mix together. Add tomatoes and toss. In separate bowl put 1 cup mayonnaise and 3 tablespoons water; whisk together. Then add BBQ sauce and Worcestershire sauce. Whisk again. Pour over macaroni mixture and mix well. Serve cold.

BETTY'S BAKED BEANS

June Zuranski

½ lb. bacon
1 med. onion, chopped
¼ green pepper, chopped
1 can baked beans
1 can butter beans

1 can kidney beans
½ c. catsup
1 tsp. mustard
½ c. brown sugar
½ c. water

Sauté bacon; cut into pieces. Drain fat, leave enough to sauté onion and green peppers. Add 3 cans of beans. Mix catsup, mustard, brown sugar and water. Pour into a casserole with beans and mix well. Bake at 350° for 1 to 1½ hours, uncovered.

BEBE'S SPINACH ARTICHOKES

Charlotte Appledorn

1 pkg. fresh spinach
1 (8-oz.) pkg. cream cheese
1 can artichoke hearts,
  quartered
6 T. butter

½ c. milk
1 lg. jar mushrooms
2 tomatoes, sliced
½ c. grated Parmesan cheese

Arrange in 9 x 13-inch casserole dish in layers: Artichokes, spinach, mushrooms and tomatoes. In blender, put cream cheese, milk and butter. Blend well. Pour blended mixture over vegetables. Sprinkle Parmesan cheese on top. Bake at 350° for ½ hour or until hot and top is brown and bubbly.

34808-00

BROCCOLI AND RICE

Shirley Cote

2 pkgs. frozen chopped broccoli
2 c. cooked rice, firm
1 (8-oz.) jar Cheez Whiz
1/4 c. margarine
1 c. chopped onion

1 c. chopped celery
1 can cream of chicken soup
1 can cream of celery soup
1/2 c. milk
Salt & pepper to taste

Sauté onion and celery in margarine. Add soups, milk and Cheez Whiz. Mix in rice and broccoli. Put in casserole. Bake or freeze to cook at a later date. Use canned onion rings, croutons, cheese or bread crumbs on top. Bake at 350° for 1 hour.

BROCCOLI BAKE

Janet Schenone

White rice, cooked
Broccoli
2 sm. cans sliced mushrooms

1 can cream of mushroom soup
Grated cheddar cheese

Place a 1/2 to 1-inch layer of cooked rice in bottom of baking dish. Prepare broccoli to crisp stage and save water. Drain mushrooms and save juice from cans. Sprinkle broccoli and mushrooms over rice. Combine water and juice reserves with cream of mushroom soup. Pour soup mixture over rice and broccoli and sprinkle with cheddar cheese. Bake 1/2 hour at 325° or until bubbly.

BROCCOLI A LA L.W.R.

Anonymous

20 oz. frozen chopped broccoli
1/4 stick butter or margarine

1/2 lb. shredded Velveeta cheese

Topping:

1/2 stick butter

1 tube crushed Ritz crackers

Cook broccoli 5 minutes and drain very well. Melt 1/2 stick butter and cheese together. Mix with broccoli. Melt 1/2 stick butter and mix 1 tube crushed crackers. Pour over top of broccoli and bake 30 minutes in 350° oven.

Recipe Favorites

34808-00

Main Dishes & Casseroles

Helpful Hints

- When preparing a casserole, make an additional batch to freeze. It makes a great emergency meal when unexpected guests arrive. Just take the casserole from the freezer and bake it in the oven.

- To keep hot oil from splattering, sprinkle a little salt or flour in the pan before frying.

- Never overcook foods that are to be frozen. Foods will finish cooking when reheated. Don't refreeze cooked thawed foods.

- A few drops of lemon juice added to simmering rice will keep the grains separated.

- Green pepper may change the flavor of frozen casseroles. Clove, garlic and pepper flavors get stronger when they are frozen, while sage, onion and salt get milder.

- Don't freeze cooked egg whites; they become tough.

- Spray your grill with vegetable oil to prevent sticking.

- Instant potatoes are a good stew thickener.

- When freezing foods, label each container with its contents and the date it was put into the freezer. Store at 0°. Always use frozen cooked foods within one to two months.

- Store dried pasta, rice (except brown rice) and whole grains in tightly covered containers in a cool, dry place. Always refrigerate brown rice, and refrigerate or freeze grains if they will not be used within five months.

- Glazed pottery, earthenware, glass, metal - all can be used for casseroles. Many of these casserole containers come in bright colors and pleasing designs to complement your tableware. The type of container you use makes very little difference, as long as it is heatproof.

- Soufflé dishes are designed with straight sides to help your soufflé climb to magnificent heights. Ramekins are good for serving individual casseroles.

- To keep boiled lasagna noodles from sticking together as they cool, keep the noodles separate by draping them over the rim of a pot.

Main Dishes & Casseroles

PAELLA

Lorraine Mondulick

2 T. olive oil
1½ lbs. chicken legs, cut into
thighs & drumsticks
½ lb. chorizo or spicy sausage,
sliced ½ inch
1 med. onion, finely chopped
2 cloves garlic, minced
2 c. uncooked rice
2 (14½-oz.) cans chicken broth
1 (16-oz.) can crushed tomatoes

⅛ tsp. saffron
¼ tsp. salt
¼ tsp. pepper
1 lb. med. raw shrimp, shelled &
deveined
1 doz. mussels or clams,
scrubbed
1 (10-oz.) pkg. frozen peas,
thawed

Heat oil in Dutch oven or Paella pan. Cook chicken on all sides until browned. Set aside. Cook chorizo until brown. Remove from pan. Set aside. Sauté onion and garlic until tender. Add rice. Stir to coat. Stir in broth, tomatoes, saffron, salt, pepper, chicken and chorizo. Bring to a boil. Reduce heat. Cover; simmer 20 minutes. Add shrimp, mussels and peas to rice mixture. Cover; simmer 10 to 12 minutes or until shrimp in pink and mussels are open. Makes 8 servings.

ESTAPADO

Pauline H. Vachon

1 lb. lean beef, cut into 1-inch
cubes
1 T. oil
1 c. dry red wine
1 (8-oz.) can tomatoes
1 lg. onion, sliced
1 green bell pepper, cut in strips
½ c. sliced fresh mushrooms
¼ c. sliced ripe olives
¼ c. raisins

½ c. dried apricots, halves
1 clove garlic, minced
1½ tsp. salt
⅛ tsp. pepper
1 tsp. dried basil
1 tsp. dried tarragon
1 bay leaf
1 tsp. thyme
1 T. flour
¾-1 c. cold water

In a large skillet, brown meat in hot oil. Add red wine, tomatoes, onion, bell pepper, raisins, apricots, garlic, salt and pepper. In a cheesecloth tie the basil, thyme, tarragon and bay leaf; together and add to skillet. Simmer, covered 1 hour. Add mushrooms and olives; simmer 30 minutes more. Discard cheesecloth with spices. Combine flour and water; stir into stew. Cook, stirring constantly, until mixture thickens and bubbles. Serve over cooked rice or risotto. Serves 6 to 8.

CHOP SUEY

Angela Smith

1½ lbs. lean pork, cut into
  1½-inch strips
1 c. sliced fresh mushrooms
3 T. shortening
1 c. sliced onions
1½ c. sliced celery
1 tsp. ginger
½ tsp. salt & pepper
2 chicken bouillon cubes

2½ c. water
1-lb. can bean sprouts, drained
5-oz. can sliced water
  chestnuts, drained
5-oz. can bamboo shoots,
  drained
¼ c. cornstarch
½ c. soy sauce
6 c. cooked rice

Brown pork and mushrooms in shortening. Add onions, celery, ginger, salt, pepper, bouillon cubes and water. Simmer, stirring occasionally, 20 to 30 minutes, until meat is tender. Add bean sprouts, water chestnuts and bamboo shoots. Combine cornstarch and soy sauce; stir into mixture. Simmer 10 minutes. Serve over hot cooked rice.

SUKIYAKI

Jo Ann Dain

1 lb. thinly sliced beef
8 oz. sliced fresh mushrooms
1 bunch green onions, cut in
  1-inch pieces
1 c. sliced celery

2 med. onions, thinly sliced
1 T. olive oil
3 c. raw spinach
8-oz. pkg. firm tofu, cut into
  bite-sized cubes

Sauce:

¾ c. beef bouillon
3 tsp. sugar

¼ c. soy sauce
2 c. cooked rice

Combine beef bouillon, sugar and soy sauce. Set aside. In a deep frying pan or pot brown thinly sliced beef in oil. Add onions, celery and mushrooms and sauce. Simmer 10 minutes or until vegetables are just tender. Mix in cubed tofu. Add spinach on top. Cover and cook 5 minutes. Serve over warm cooked rice.

INDONESIAN CHICKEN SHISHKABOB

Marcie Lynn Leffent

2 chicken breasts, boneless,
  skinless & cut 1-inch sq.
1 green pepper, cut in 1-inch
  squares
1 red pepper, 1-inch squares

1 onion, lg. sliced
Soy sauce
1 T. sugar
6 bamboo skewers

Cut chicken breasts in 1-inch pieces. Marinate in soy sauce. Skewer alternately onion, red pepper, chicken, green pepper, etc. Lay skewers

(continued)

34808-00

on boiler pan and broil change sides of each skewer once during broiling. Serves 4.

BARCELONA BEEF KABOBS WITH KASHI

Jo Anne Dain

1½ lbs. boneless beef, cut into
  2-inch cubes
⅓ c. orange juice concentrate
6 oz. tomato juice
2 T. lime or lemon juice
1 T. olive oil
1 tsp. paprika
1 red bell pepper
1 med. onion

8 mushrooms
2 garlic cloves
1½ tsp. cumin
1 tsp. oregano
1 pkt. Kashi pilaf (in Publix
  health food section) or 1 c.
  rice, cooked in two c. chicken
  broth according to directions

Combine orange juice concentrate, tomato juice, lime or lemon juice, olive oil, paprika, minced garlic cloves, cumin and oregano in large bowl. Mix well. Add beef cubes and mix well. Cover and refrigerate overnight. Cut bell pepper, onion and mushrooms into bite-sized chunks. Place in frying pan. Put beef cubes on skewers and grill until done. Pour marinade over vegetables in frying pan and simmer until done. Serve over hot Kashi or rice.

BOEUF EN DAUBE

Linda Ball

3 lbs. round beef, cut into 1-inch
  cubes, no gristle or fat
2 tsp. salt
1 c. flour
1 tsp. paprika
6 strips bacon
2 cloves garlic, finely chopped
1 oz. warm brandy
12 sm. mushrooms
12 sm. carrots

12 sm. peeled white onions
6 whole peppercorns
4 whole cloves
1 bay leaf, crumbled
2 T. chopped parsley
Generous pinch of dried
  marjoram and thyme
1½ c. red wine (dry)
1 c. condensed beef bouillon

Place flour, salt and paprika in bag; add beef cubes. Shake to coat. Fry bacon in heavy iron skillet until brown not crisp. Remove and cut into 1-inch pieces and place in large casserole. In the bacon fat add garlic then leaf. Brown on all sides turning frequently. Pour brandy over meat; after a few minutes; remove meat, placing over bacon in casserole. Next brown, mushrooms, transfer to casserole. Add 1 cup bouillon, 1 cup wine and pan juices to casserole. Add onions, carrots, peppercorns, cloves, bay leaf, chopped parsley, marjoram and thyme. Pour another ½ cup wine over casserole, cover tightly and bake in a 300° oven for 3 hours.

BEEF BOURGIGNON

June Jorgensen

1½ lbs. lean beef, cut in cubes (chuck is good if very lean)
2 tsp. vegetable oil
1 (1-lb.) can tomatoes
½ c. burgundy wine
1 beef bouillon cube
1½ tsp. salt
½ tsp. basil
½ tsp. garlic salt
¼ tsp. pepper
1 sm. bay leaf
8 sm. white onions
8 young carrots, peeled & cut in quarters
2 T. cornstarch
¼ c. water

Brown beef in oil. Add tomatoes, wine, bouillon cube and seasonings. Cover and simmer for 45 minutes. Add onions and carrots. Cover and cook 45 minutes longer or until meat and vegetables are tender. Blend cornstarch and water. Stir into mixture and cook, stirring frequently, until thicken. Remove bay leaf. Serve over rice. Serves 4 to 5.

COMPANY BEEF STEW

Mary Button

2 lbs. boneless beef, cut into 2-inch cubes
¼ c. flour
2 tsp. salt
½ tsp. paprika
¼ tsp. pepper
3 T. shortening
1 c. water
8-oz. can tomato sauce
2 bouillon cubes
3 whole cloves
6 sm. onions
6 medium-sized potatoes
4 medium-sized carrots, cut in half
10-oz. pkg. frozen peas
1 c. sliced celery
1 c. water

Coat meat with mixture of flour, salt, paprika and pepper. Slowly brown in shortening in large skillet about 3 minutes. Add water, tomato sauce, bouillon cubes and cloves. Cover. Simmer 45 minutes longer. Add onions, tomatoes, carrots, peas, celery and water. Cover. Continue cooking for 15 minutes until vegetables are tender.

A MICROWAVE TASTY STEW

Sonya Smetzer

1 lb. beef for stew or boneless top sirloin, cut in sm. pieces
½ c. chopped yellow onion
1 branch diced celery
1 (16-oz.) can stewed tomatoes
1 clove minced garlic
½ tsp. thyme
½ c. water
2 c. sliced carrots
2 med. potatoes, chopped
½ c. Merlot

Combine in 3-quart casserole: meat, onion, celery and water, medium power level. Stir halfway through (if necessary, add more water). Add

(continued)

46

34808-00

carrots, potatoes and Merlot. Cover and cook 30 minutes on medium power level or until the meat is tender.

HAMBURGER STROGANOFF

Darlene Jenny

1 lb. lean ground beef
½ c. chopped onion
2 T. flour
½ tsp. salt
2 cloves garlic, minced
¼ tsp. pepper

1 (4-oz.) can mushroom stems & pieces, drained
1 (10½-oz.) can condensed cream of chicken soup
1 c. sour cream

In a large skillet cook and stir meat and onion until meat is browned and onion is tender. Drain off any excess fat. Stir in flour, salt, garlic, pepper and mushrooms. Cook 5 minutes stirring constantly. Stir in soup, heat to boiling and stir constantly. Reduce heat, simmer uncovered 10 minutes. Stir in sour cream and heat through but to not boil. Serve over egg noodles. Serves 4.

CHEESE STEAK

Janet Schenone

1-lb thin steak
8 oz. sliced mozzarella cheese
Sm. jar spaghetti sauce
Salt

Pepper
Flour
Oil

Salt and pepper steak and roll in flour. Fry steak quickly in small amount of oil. Thin spaghetti sauce with small amount of water and put thin layer in bottom of baking dish. Place fried pieces of steak in dish and cover lightly with sauce. Cover and bake 30 to 45 minutes at 350°. Uncover and place layer of mozzarella cheese on top. Bake 5 to 10 minutes longer or until cheese melts. Serve with spaghetti and remaining sauce.

CROCKPOT SPAGHETTI SAUCE

Darlene Jenny

1 lb. lean ground beef
1 lg. onion, chopped
2 cloves garlic, minced
2 (1-lb.) cans tomatoes, cut up
1 (8-oz.) can tomato sauce
1 (12-oz.) can tomato paste
1 c. beef bouillon

2 T. minced parsley
1 T. brown sugar
1 tsp. dried oregano
1 tsp. dried basil leaves
1 tsp. salt
¼ tsp. pepper

Combine ground beef with onion and garlic in a large skillet. Break up pieces of meat with fork and cook until it loses its red color. Drain off

(continued)

excess fat. In a slow cooking pot (crockpot), combine browned meat, onions and garlic with all remaining ingredients. Cover and cook on low for 6 to 8 hours. Serve over hot spaghetti.

SURPRISE MEAT LOAF

Sandy True

1½ lbs. ground beef
1 c. med. bread crumbs
½ c. cornflakes, crushed
⅔ c. diced cheese
½ c. chopped onion
½ c. diced celery

2 T. diced green pepper
1 tsp. salt
Dash garlic powder
2 beaten eggs
1 (8-oz.) can tomato sauce
2 T. catsup

Combine all ingredients except the catsup. Shape and place in loaf pan (9-inch). Score top of loaf with back of table knife. Bake at 350° for 30 minutes. Remove from oven and fill lines with catsup. Continue baking 30 to 40 minutes longer. Serves 8. Also good cold.

FIESTA MEAT LOAF

Mary Button

½ c. chopped onion
½ c. chopped celery
½ c. chopped green pepper
2 T. butter
1 (12-oz.) bottle Heinz chili
  sauce

1½ lbs. lean ground beef
1 c. soft bread crumbs
1 egg, slightly beaten
½ tsp. salt
¼ tsp. pepper

Sauté onion, celery and green pepper in butter until tender. Stir in chili sauce. Combine ½ of mixture with ground beef, bread crumbs, eggs, salt and pepper. Form into a loaf in shallow baking dish. Bake at 350° for 1 hour. Let stand 5 minutes before slicing.

"MY FAVORITE" CHILI

Robert J. Woyciechowski

1 lb. ground round
1¼ c. chopped onion
2½ c. dark red kidney beans
1⅓ c. condensed tomato soup
1⅓ c. whole milk

1½-2 tsp. chili powder
1 T. flour
1 tsp. salt
3 tsp. water

Cook ground round and onion until brown in 3 tablespoons of butter. In separate kettle mix milk, kidney beans and tomato soup. Cook about 10 minutes. Then add beef and onion mixture. Take chili powder, flour, salt and water; make into a paste and blend in. Cook over low heat, stirring frequently for 45 minutes.

48

34808-00

CHILE

Dorothy Scheuer

½-1 lb. lean ground beef
1 onion, chopped
2 carrots, chopped
1 green pepper, chopped
2 stalks celery, chopped
2 garlic cloves, chopped
4-5 red potatoes, diced
1 can vegetable broth

1 (18-oz.) can chopped tomatoes
1 (6-oz.) can can tomato paste
2 cans whole kernel corn
1 can kidney beans, drained
1 can northern beans
1 pkg. mild chili seasoning mix
1 tsp. sugar
Water, as needed

Sauté beef and drain. Soften vegetables in water in microwave. Combine all ingredients in large crockpot or soup pot. Cook on high 2 to 3 hours and simmer until ready to serve. The longer the better.

NUKE CHILI

Sonya Smetzer

1 lb. ground turkey
1 can dark red kidney beans
1 can Ro-Tel tomatoes & chilies
1 can tomato soup

1 branch celery, chopped
⅒ lg. yellow onion, chopped
1 T. chili powder
Grated cheese

Put turkey in a 3-quart casserole dish, cook on high power for about 5 minutes. Add beans, tomatoes and chilies, tomato soup, celery, onion and chili powder. Cook 30 to 40 minutes on high power, stirring on occasion. This Nuke Chili tastes best the second day after the flavors have blended. Serve with grated cheese on top, crackers or taco chips.

TURKISH TURKEY TACOS

Jo Anne Dain

1 lb. ground turkey
1 T. olive oil
½ c. chopped onion
¼ c. slivered almonds or
  chopped pecans
¼ c. raisins
¼ c. red wine or chicken broth

1 c. plain yogurt (opt.)
1½ tsp. cumin
½ tsp. oregano
¼ tsp. cinnamon
¼ tsp. nutmeg
¼ tsp. pepper
8 flour tortillas

Cook chopped onion in in olive oil. Add cumin, oregano, cinnamon, nutmeg and pepper. Mix well. Stir in crumbled turkey and wine or broth and cook until light done (about 10 minutes). Add raisins and nuts. Simmer on low heat for 5 minutes, adding more liquid, if necessary. Serve taco-style on warm flour tortillas. Serve yogurt on the side as an optional topping.

CHICKEN POT PIE

Pauline H. Vachon

4 T. margarine or butter
5 T. flour
1 c. chicken broth
½ c. white wine
½ c. evaporated milk

Salt & pepper to taste
1 c. frozen or fresh carrots & peas
1 pie shell for top

In a medium saucepan melt margarine, then add flour and cook until frothy. Add chicken broth, wine, evaporated milk, salt and pepper; cook until mixture thickens. Add chicken and vegetables, pour into 9-inch pan. Top with pie crust, brush with milk, make 3 or 4 slits on top. Bake at 450° for 15 minutes, then 350° for 20 to 30 minutes until crust is golden.

EASY CHICKEN POT PIE

Leslie McQueen

1⅔ c. frozen mixed vegetables, thawed
1 c. cut-up cooked chicken
1 (10¼ oz.) condensed cream of chicken soup

1 c. Bisquick original OR reduced fat baking mix
½ c. milk
1 egg

Preheat oven to 400°. Mix vegetables, chicken and soup. Stir in Bisquick, milk and egg. In an ungreased 9-inch pie plate pour all ingredients. Bake 30 minutes or until golden brown. Serve 6.

CHICKEN POPPY SEED

Rhonda Maule

1 whole boiled chicken, deboned or 6 chicken breasts
2 cans cream of chicken soup
1 (16 oz.) sour cream

1 box Ritz crackers
2 sticks butter
2 T. poppy seed

Mix chicken, soup and sour cream together in bowl. In separate bowl mix last 3 ingredients. In 13 x 9-inch glass dish, put a layer of the cracker mix on bottom (½ of mixture). Cover with remaining half of cracker mix on top. Cook at 350° for 40 minutes until brown on top.

PARMESAN CHICKEN

Leslie McQueen

4 chicken breasts, skinned
1 c. bread crumbs
¾ tsp. salt
1 T. parsley flakes

½ c. melted butter
⅓ c. Parmesan cheese
½ tsp. garlic powder

(continued)

34808-00

Coat chicken well in butter and then mixture. Bake at 350° for approximately 1 hour. **Do not cover.**

CHICKEN A LA KING

Roberta Barbaro

1 (10-oz.) pkg. puff pastry shells
½ c. diced green pepper
2 tsp. butter or margarine
1 c. cream of chicken soup

½ c. milk
2 c. cubed, cooked chicken or turkey
¼ c. diced pimento

Bake pastry shells according to package directions. In medium saucepan, cook pepper in butter until tender. Add soup, milk, chicken and pimiento. Heat, stirring occasionally. Spoon into warm pastry shells. Makes 6 servings.

TACO RO-TEL CHICKEN CASSEROLE

Debbie Becker

2 cans cream of chicken soup
1 lg. fryer, boiled & deboned OR
  6 boneless chicken breasts, cooked
1 lg. onion

½ stick margarine
1 bag Doritos
1 can Ro-Tel tomatoes
½ lb. sharp cheddar cheese

Sauté onions in butter. Add Ro-Tel tomatoes (after blending in blender) to onions. Add soup and cheese to mixture and mix well. Then add Doritos and cooked chicken pieces. Stir well and top with more cheese. Bake at 350° for 30 minutes.

LUCKY CHICKEN

Peggy Donaldson

2 boneless, skinless chicken breasts
1 T. melted butter or margarine
½ c. chopped celery*

½ c. chopped red pepper*
½ c. chopped green pepper*
½ c. chopped onion

*Substitute vegetables as desired. Cut up and brown chicken. Add vegetables

Make Sauce:

2 T. brown sugar
1 c. ketchup

1 c. water

Mix and pour over chicken. Simmer, covered, 30 minutes. Serve over rice or noodles.

CHICKEN RICE-A-RONI

Angela Smith

1 pkg. chicken Rice-A-Roni
1 chicken, cooked & deboned
3½ c. chicken broth (hot)
Sm. bell pepper, chopped
Sm. onion, chopped

1 can cream of celery soup
½ c. grated cheddar cheese
Sm. can Durkee French-fried
  onions
1 T. butter

Sauté pepper and onion in a 1 tablespoon butter. Add Rice-A-Roni and cook as directed on package using chicken broth for water. Add chicken and soup after Rice-A-Roni is cooked. Mix well and place in casserole dish. Grate cheese on top and sprinkle with onions. Cook at 350° until cheese is melted.

CHICKEN CASSEROLE

Selda Berns

Chicken breasts for 6
2 cans Campbell's golden
  mushroom soup
½ can water

1 c. white wine
Baby carrots
Celery pieces

Spices (sprinkle):

Onion salt
Garlic salt
Oregano

Minced onion
Pepper

Wash chicken and sprinkle with spices. Place in large pot. Pour on soup, wine and water. Put in carrots and celery pieces. Cover pot. Turn flame to medium and cook for 1½ hours. Needs no stirring. Serve over noodles or rice.

AUTUMN NOODLE BAKE FOR TWO

Leslie McQueen

4 oz. UNcooked wide egg
  noodles
1 c. diced, cooked chicken,
  turkey OR ham
1 (10½-oz.) condensed cream of
  mushroom soup

1 can shredded cheddar cheese
1 (8¼-oz.) can sliced carrots,
  drained
1 (8-oz.) can green beans,
  drained

Cook noodles according to package directions. Combine noodles with chicken, soup, ½ cup of water or milk, vegetables and ½ cup of shredded cheddar cheese. Spoon into a 2-quart baking dish. Top with remaining cheese. Bake uncovered at 350° for 20 minutes or until heated through and cheese is melted.

34808-00

CHICKEN MACARONI CASSEROLE

Martha Swift

1 (7-oz.) pkg. elbow macaroni
2 slices bacon
2 cans cream of mushroom
  soup
3/4 c. milk
2 T. vinegar

2 tsp. sugar
1 med. garlic clove, minced
2 cans chunk chicken
1 c. sliced cooked carrots
1 c. shredded cheddar cheese
1 c. cooked peas

Prepare noodles. In 10-inch skillet over medium heat, cook bacon until crisp, remove and crumble. Stir soup, milk, vinegar, sugar and garlic into drippings. In large bowl combine soup mixture and remaining ingredients. Pour mixture into 2½-quart casserole cover. Bake at 350° for 30 minutes. Serves many.

MACARONI AND CHEESE DELUXE

Audrey Millican

1 (8 oz.) Muellers ready-cut
  macaroni
2 c. cream-style cottage cheese
1 (8-oz.) ctn. sour cream
1 egg, slightly beaten

¾ tsp. salt
Dash of white pepper
2 c. grated cheddar cheese
Paprika

Cook macaroni, drain and rinse well. Combine cottage cheese, sour cream, egg, salt and pepper, grated cheddar cheese. Add macaroni, blend. Spoon into 2-quart casserole. Sprinkle with paprika. Bake at 350° for 45 minutes. Excellent side dish with any meat. Can be frozen and baked later.

CHICKEN NOODLE CASSEROLE

Michelle Logan

1 (10-oz.) pkg. noodles
2 c. chicken broth
1 can cream of mushroom soup

½ can water
1 whole chicken, cut up
1 pkg. onion soup mix

Grease small roaster. Put uncooked noodles on bottom. Cover with cut-up chicken. Pour broth over chicken. Mix mushroom soup and water and pour over. Sprinkle onion soup mix over top. Cover and bake 2 hours at 350°.

RUSH-HOUR SIMMER DINNER

Martha Swift

4 (5½-oz.) bundles nested vermicelli pasta
2 (6¾-oz.) cans chunk-style chicken
1 c. frozen peas

1 (8-oz.) can whole small carrots
1 sm. onion, thinly sliced
1¼ c. chicken broth
1 tsp. dried tarragon

In 10-inch skillet arrange the pasta, undrained chicken, frozen peas, carrots and sliced onion. Add the chicken broth and sprinkle with tarragon. Bring to boiling, reduce heat. Cover and simmer for 15 to 20 minutes or until noodles are just tender.

MEXICAN CHICKEN
(Microwave)

Marcie Lynn Leffent

1 med. green pepper, thinly sliced
1 sm. onion, sliced & separate into rings
8 oz. mushrooms, sliced
1 c. (4 oz.) chopped green chiles, drained

2 whole bone-in chicken breasts, halved
¼ tsp. chili powder
¼ tsp. oregano
⅛ tsp. garlic powder
1 (15-oz.) can tomato sauce or 2 sm. cans

In 12 x 8-inch baking dish, combine green pepper, onion, mushrooms and chilies. Cover. Microwave on high 4-5 minutes, until pepper is tender-crisp. Stir once. Drain. Arrange chicken breasts, bone-side up, nearest position to outside of dish. Combine spices and tomato sauce. Pour over breast. Cover. Microwave on high 10 to 16 minutes. Turn oven. Add remaining sauce and cover at half time. Serves 4.

CHICKEN MEXICANO

Shirley Grube

1 T. butter
1 (8-oz.) pkg. nacho-flavor chips
4-6 chicken breasts, cooked & cut into bite-size pieces
2 (10¾-oz.) cans cream of chicken soup

3 T. mild salsa
1 c. fat-free sour cream
2½ c. shredded Monterey Jack cheese

Butter a 3-quart (9 x 13-inch) casserole dish. Place taco chips on bottom of dish. Top chips with chicken. In a large bowl, combine soup, salsa and sour cream. Mix well and spread over chicken covering all surfaces. Sprinkle cheese over the top. Bake at 350° for ½ hour or until cheese is melted and mixture is bubbling.

34808-00

SPINACH AND CHICKEN ENCHILADAS

1½ lbs. chicken breast,
  boneless, skinless, cooked &
  diced
¼ c. chopped onion
1 (10-oz.) pkg. frozen, chopped
  spinach
1 T. butter, melted
1 (10¾-oz.) can cream of
  chicken soup

¾ c. milk
1 (4-oz.) can green chilies
1 (8-oz.) ctn. sour cream
3 c. (12 oz.) shredded Monterey
  Jack cheese, divided
8 flour tortillas

Cook spinach according to package; drain well and reserve 1 cup broth. Set aside. Sauté onion in butter until tender in large saucepan. Stir in ¾ of spinach and all of chicken; set aside. Combine soup, reserved spinach broth, milk, green chilies, sour cream and half of cheese in a bowl; mix well. Stir half of sauce mixture into chicken mixture. Reserve remaining sauce. Spoon chicken mixture evenly down center of each tortilla; roll up tortillas and place seam side down in 2 (9 x 9 x 2-inch) pans. For spicer enchiladas use 4 fresh chopped jalapeños. Pour remaining sauce over enchiladas. Bake at 350° for 25 minutes. Sprinkle with remaining cheese. Bake an additional 5 to 10 minutes.

MOROCCAN STEW

Shirley Grube

2 tsp. vegetable oil
2 c. chopped onion
2 lg. cloves garlic, crushed
1 c. carrots, sliced crosswise ⅛
  inch thick
1 lg. green bell pepper, cut into
  ¼-inch strips
1 tsp. ground cumin
½ tsp. each ground allspice,
  ground ginger & turmeric
¼ tsp. each salt & cayenne
  pepper

¼ tsp. ground cinnamon
¾ c. water
1 med. eggplant, peeled & cut
  into ¼-inch cubes (4 c.)
3 lg., ripe tomatoes, chopped (3
  c.)
½ c. raisins
1 (1-lb.) can chickpeas, rinsed &
  drained or 2 c. cooked
  chickpeas

Heat oil in a large saucepan over medium heat. Add onion and garlic. Cook, stirring occasionally, 3 minutes. Add carrots, bell pepper, spices and ¼ cup of the water. Cook, stirring occasionally 5 minutes. Add eggplant, tomatoes, raisins, chickpeas and rest of water until vegetables are tender. Stir several times during cooking. Serve over couscous rice or any cooked grain.

CHEESE 'N SPINACH CASSEROLE

Sandy True

1-lb. ctn. creamy cottage cheese
3 med. eggs
¼ c. butter or margarine
¼ lb. American cheese,
  coarsely cut

1 pkg. chopped frozen spinach,
  thawed & drained
3 T. flour
¼ tsp. salt
Dash of garlic powder (opt.)

Put cottage cheese in large mixing bowl. Add unbeaten eggs, cheese and butter; cut into coarse pieces, chopped spinach, flour and salt. Stir to blend well. Pour into buttered 1½-quart casserole dish. Bake at 350° until set, about 45 minutes.

EGGPLANT PARMESAN

Shirley Grube

1 eggplant
½ lb. sliced mozzarella cheese
2 tomatoes, sliced thin
½ lb. mushrooms, sliced

¼ c. oil
½ c. bread crumbs
1 egg
1 c. tomato sauce

Peel eggplant and slice in ½-inch rounds. Pound with mallet to ¼-inch thickness. Dip slices in egg, then bread crumbs. Sauté eggplant in oil. Drain on paper towels. Place eggplant in bottom of 10 x 10-inch oven baking dish. Arrange tomato slices on eggplant the sliced mushrooms. Top with tomato sauce. Arrange mozzarella cheese over top. Bake at 450° for 15 to 20 minutes.

BAKED ZITI

Barbara Davis

1 (16-oz.) box ziti
16 oz. cottage cheese
½ c. Parmesan cheese
24 oz. mozzarella cheese
½ c. red wine
2 lbs. ground beef

2 lg. eggs
Fresh parsley, chopped
Onion & garlic
Salt & pepper
2 lg. jars spaghetti sauce

Mix ¾ of mozzarella, ¼ cup Parmesan, cottage cheese, red wine, eggs, parsley, onion, garlic, salt and pepper together in large bowl. Brown beef and drain well. Cook ziti al dente. Mix beef, ziti and cheese mixture together with spaghetti sauce. Sprinkle rest of Parmesan and mozzarella over top. Makes 1 large casserole or 2 small ones. Bake at 350° for 35 minutes.

34808-00

PUERTO RICAN LASAGNA

Judith Grant

4 ripe/sweet plantains with
  brown skin
2 tomatoes, chopped
1 chopped onion
3 cloves garlic
1 ea. red & green pepper
1 sm. tomato paste
1-lb. can chopped beef
1 lb. mozzarella cheese,
  shredded

1 c. Parmesan cheese
2 T. butter
1 beef/chicken bouillon
4 T. olive oil
1 tsp. thyme
1 tsp. oregano
Salt & pepper to taste

Cut plantains elongated ovals and fry in oil until golden brown. Drain on napkin. Brown chopped beef and drain. Remove meat and sauté onion in butter and oil. Add mashed and chopped peppers, garlic, chopped tomatoes and spices. Add bouillon. Add tomato paste to mixture and simmer. Add meat and simmer. In lasagna pan: Add 1 layer of plantains. Place meat over plantains, then mozzarella cheese, then sauce. Repeat. Last layer is plantains, then mozzarella cheese and Parmesan cheese. Heat in oven at 350° for 25 minutes until cheese is golden.

GREEN AND WHITE LASAGNE

Michelle Winter

½ lb. lasagne noodles
1 tub ricotta cheese
½ c. fresh Parmesan cheese
¼ c. extra virgin olive oil
2 yellow onions, thinly sliced
4 zucchini, trimmed and thinly
  sliced, crosswise
Salt & pepper
Freshly grated nutmeg

1 lb. fresh mushrooms
3 cloves garlic, minced
¼ c. unsalted butter
¼ c. all-purpose flour
3 c. milk
40 fresh basil leaves
½ lb. whole milk mozzarella,
  shredded

Cook lasagne according to package directions. When lasagne is done. Drain and set aide. In a small bowl, combine ricotta, Parmesan and salt and pepper to taste until well mixed. Set aside. In a large frying pan over medium heat, sauté onion in olive oil until soft. Add zucchini, mushrooms and garlic; cook until all are tender. Season with salt and pepper to taste. Set aside. In a saucepan over low heat, melt butter. Whisk in flour and cook, stirring, for 2 minutes. Gradually whisk in milk until sauce is smooth and thickened, 3 to 4 minutes. Season with salt and pepper and nutmeg to taste. Oil a 9 x 13-inch baking dish. Preheat oven to 375°. Cover bottom of baking dish with layer of noodles. Spoon ⅓ cup ricotta mixture over top. Sprinkle ⅓ of vegetables over ricotta layer and cover with ⅓ white sauce mixture. Distribute ⅓ of basil leaves

(continued)

evenly over sauce. Repeat layers ending with basil. Sprinkle mozzarella cheese evenly over top. Bake 30 to 40 minutes. Let cool briefly.

LASAGNA ROLLS

Martha Swift

1 tsp. salad oil
1 med. onion, finely chopped
1 (28-oz.) Italian plus tomatoes
1 (6-oz.) can tomato paste
2 tsp. sugar
½ tsp. Italian herb seasonings

½ (16-oz.) pkg. curly lasagna
  noodles (about 9)
1 (10-oz.) pkg. chopped spinach
1 (15 oz.) ricotta cheese
2 T. Parmesan cheese

Prepare Sauce: In nonstick 10-inch skillet over medium heat, in hot salad oil, cook onion until tender. Add tomatoes with their liquid, tomato paste, sugar, Italian herb seasonings, ½ teaspoon salt and ¾ cup water over high heat heating to boiling. Stirring to break up tomatoes. Reduce heat to low, cover and simmer sauce 15 minutes stirring occasionally. Meanwhile, prepare lasagna noodles as label directs. Prepare oven to 375°. Spoon sauce into shallow 2½-quart casserole or 13 x 9-inch glass baking dish. In bowl mix spinach, ricotta cheese, Parmesan cheese, pepper and ¾ teaspoon salt until blended. Spread rounded ¼ cup ricotta filling on each noodle and roll jelly roll-fashion. With serrated knife slice each rolled noodle crosswise in half. Arrange rolls, cut-side down in sauce in casserole in 1 layer. Cover dish loosely with foil. Bake 35 to 40 minutes until hot and bubbly. Makes 8 main-dish servings.

MANICOTTI - CREPES AND FILLING

Jo Russo

Crepes:

1 c. milk
1 c. flour

5 eggs
¼ tsp. salt

Filling:

3 lbs. ricotta
2 eggs
1 lb. mozzarella cheese,
  shredded
3 T. grated cheese

¼ tsp. garlic powder
2 T. parsley, chopped
Salt & pepper to taste
Dash of nutmeg

Beat eggs in bowl, gradually add flour, milk and salt. In a small frying pan greased with butter, pour about 3 tablespoons of mixture. Cook one side only, flip cooked side up on waxed paper. Spoon mixture, 2 tablespoons into crepe and roll. Cover bottom of baking pan with sauce. Place manicotti in pan. Cover them with sauce. Bake at 350° for 20 to 30 minutes.

34808-00

MANICOTTI A LA FRANCIS

Janet Barry

1 c. flour
1 egg
1 tsp. salt
1 c. mllk
1 T. oil
1 lb. ricotta cheese

½ c. grated cheese Parmesan
  or Romano
Salt & pepper to taste
1 egg
1 tsp. dried or fresh parsley

Mix 1 cup flour, 1 teaspoon salt together. Make a well and add 1 cup milk and 1 tablespoon oil and 1 egg. Gently add liquid to dry ingredients. If batter is lumpy use an egg beater for 1 minute. Set aside. Take 1-pound container for ricotta cheese and place in a large bowl. Add and mix in ½ cup grated cheese, salt, pepper and 1 egg, beaten slightly. Put in 1 teaspoon fresh or dried parsley. Mix all together. Heat up a 8⅓-inch crepe pan with some oil. Pour some of the flour batter in the pan and move pan so batter covers bottoms of pan. Cook 1 minute Don't allow batter to burn. Take pancake and fill with ricotta filling (1 to 2 tablespoons of filling) and roll up. Place folded side down into a pan with some prepared red sauce on the bottom of pan. Continue to fill bottom of pan with pancakes. Layer them on top of each other by pulling some sauce between layers. End with sauce and sprinkle some grated cheese on top. Cover with foil; bake at 350° for 20 minutes. Serves 4 people.

EASY PASTA SKILLET

Janet Schenone

1 lb. ground beef
3 c. uncooked pasta (your
  choice)
1 (26-to 28-oz.) jar spaghetti
  sauce

1 (8-oz.) pkg. mozzarella cheese,
  shredded
½ c. grated Parmesan cheese

Brown ground beef in large skillet and drain excess fat. Add 2½ cups water to skillet and bring to a boil. Reduce heat to medium-low and stir in pasta. Cover skillet and simmer 10 to 5 minutes or until pasta is tender. Stir in spaghetti sauce and 1 cup of the mozzarella cheese. Sprinkle remaining cup of mozzarella and ½ cup Parmesan cheese on top. Cover skillet and cook long enough for cheese to melt.

PIEROGI CASSEROLE

Helen Cueto

4 med. potatoes, boiled &
  mashed
1½ sticks margarine
¾ lb. shredded or grated
  cheddar cheese

2 c. onion, diced fine
1 pkg. frozen spinach, thawed
8 oz. cottage cheese
1 lb. lasagna noodles, cooked
  according to directions

Add cheese to hot mashed potatoes and beat well. Sauté onions in margarine until soft. Add ⅓ of onion mixture to potatoes. Salt to taste. Butter 9 x 13-inch pan. Place layer of noodles, layer of potato, ½ of cottage cheese, of noodles, layer of potatoes, ½ of cottage cheese. Repeat, ending with noodles. Pour remaining butter and onions over top. Cover with foil. Bake at 350° until heated through; 30 minutes; let stand a few minutes, then serve in squares. Serves 8.

HAM CASSEROLE

Helen Cueto

½ c. butter or margarine
½ c. flour
2 c. milk
1 onion, cubed

1 pepper, cubed
2½-3 c. cubed ham
1 c. Swiss or cheddar cheese
3½ c. raw cubed potatoes

Brown butter or margarine, and flour. Add milk, stir until thick; set aside. Add pepper, ham, cheese to flour mixture. In bottom of baking dish (buttered), add cubed potatoes. Add ham mixture. Cover and bake in 350° oven for 30 minutes. Uncover and bake 40 minutes more. Let stand 15 minutes. Serve. (Great for leftover ham.)

EASY SHRIMP CREOLE
(Microwave)

Marcie Lynn Leffent

1 (16-oz.) can tomatoes
1 med. onion, chopped
1 green pepper, chopped
½ tsp. salt
¼ tsp. pepper
¼ tsp. basil leaves

½ tsp. chili powder
Dash cayenne
1 med. bay leaf
1 lb. fresh shrimp, shelled &
  deveined

Combine all ingredients except shrimp in 1½-quart casserole, breaking up tomatoes cover microwave on high 8 to 12 minutes until green pepper is tender. Stir once. Stir in shrimp. Cover; microwave on high 3 to 5 minutes until shrimp is opaque, stirring once or twice. **Do not overcook!** Let stand 3 to 5 minutes. Remove bay leaf. Serves 4.

34808-00

CRAB-ZUCCHINI CASSEROLE

Susan Moore

1¼ lbs. zucchini (about 5 med.)
1 med. onion, chopped
½ stick butter
½ tsp. salt
Dash of pepper
3 med. tomatoes, coarsely cut

2 cloves garlic
1 (7½-oz.) can crabmeat
1⅓ c. sm. match-like sticks
   Swiss cheese
1 tsp. sweet basil leaves
1 c. bread crumbs

Wash unpeeled zucchini and cut into ½-inch slices. Sauté with chopped onion in 2 tablespoons of butter, but do not brown. Add salt and pepper. Sauté garlic and crabmeat briefly in remaining 2 tablespoons. Discard garlic. Fold crabmeat into zucchini-onion mixture. Add cheese, tomatoes, basil and bread crumbs; toss. Pour into greased 2-quart casserole. Bake uncovered, in moderate (350°) oven for 30 minutes. Serves 8.

BACON AND EGG BAKE

Aline Grojean

6 bacon slices
2 med. onions, sliced
1 can cream of mushroom soup
  (condensed)
¼ o. milk

5 hard-boiled eggs, sliced
2 c. (8 oz.) shredded cheddar
   cheese
Dash of salt & pepper
English muffins, split, toasted

Heat oven to 350°. Fry bacon until crisp and remove from skillet. Drain fat, reserving 2 tablespoons. Sauté onions in bacon fat. Stir in soup, milk, eggs, cheese and seasonings. Pour into 10 x 6-inch baking dish. Then top with crumbled bacon. Bake at 350° for 20 minutes. Serve over muffin halves. Serves 6 to 8.

SWISS CHEESE SCRAMBLE

Susan Moore

8 pieces bacon, fried crisp,
   drained & crumbled
2 c. soft bread cubes, no crusts
1¾ c. milk
8 slightly beaten eggs
¾ tsp. salt

⅛ tsp. pepper
2 T. butter or margarine
¼ tsp. seasoned salt
½ lb. Swiss cheese, sliced
2 T. melted butter
½ c. fine, dry bread crumbs

Combine bread cubes and milk. Drain after 5 minutes. Combine drained milk with eggs, salt and pepper. Melt the butter in a frying pan. Add egg mixture and scramble until soft, not fully cooked. Add soaked bread cubes and turn into a 9-inch square or round shallow baking dish. Sprinkle with seasoned salt. Arrange the Swiss cheese over the top. Combine the melted butter and dry bread crumbs and sprinkle over cheese. Top with crumbled bacon. Bake in a hot oven (400°) for 10 to

(continued)

15 minutes until the cheese bubbles around the edge of the dish and cheese at center is melted. Serves 8.

MUSHROOM FRITTATA

Jane Goodrich

1 c. sliced fresh mushrooms
⅔ c. chopped onion
⅔ c. chopped green pepper
1 c. chopped zucchini
1 tsp. minced garlic
2 T. butter OR oil
6 lg. eggs

⅓ c. half & half
½ tsp. salt
⅛ tsp. pepper
1½ c. soft bread cube
1 (8 oz.) cream cheese
1 c. grated cheddar cheese

Sauté mushrooms, onion, green pepper, zucchini and garlic in butter. Beat eggs and half & half; add salt and pepper. Cut cream cheese into ½-inch cubes. Fold in gently to the eggs: the cooked vegetables, bread cubes, grated cheddar and the cream cheese cubes. Pour entire mixture into a greased 9-inch pie pan. Bake in a preheated oven at 350° for 45 minutes.

MUSHROOM AND ASPARAGUS STRATA

Claire Akey

1 lb. thin asparagus spears
1 T. olive oil
4 c. sliced fresh variety
  mushrooms
2 cloves garlic, minced
2 c. shredded Swiss or Edam
  cheese
2 T. fresh dill weed or 1 tsp.
  dried

12 slices French bread, cut into
  2 x 1 x 1-inch sticks
6 eggs
2¼ c. half-and-half
¼ c. grated Parmesan
Salt & pepper to taste

Cut asparagus into 3-inch pieces. Microwave for about 3 minutes. Rinse with cold water. Drain. Heat oil in large skillet. Cook mushrooms, garlic, salt and pepper for 4 to 5 minutes until liquid has evaporated. Set aside. Combine shredded cheese and dill weed. Arrange half the bread in bottom of lightly greased 2-quart baking dish. Top with half mushrooms, half cheese mixture and half asparagus. Repeat layers. Beat eggs and half-and-half. Pour mixture over layers in dish. Press slightly with back of spoon to moisten bread. Sprinkle Parmesan over top. Cover and chill 2 to 24 hours. Bake at 375° uncovered, for 45 minutes or until knife inserted in center comes out clean. Remove from oven. Let stand about 10 minutes. Cut into 6 to 8 portions to serve.

34808-00

Meat, Poultry & Seafood

Helpful Hints

- Use little oil when preparing sauces and marinades for red meats. Fat from the meat will render out during cooking and will provide plenty of flavor. Certain meats, like ribs, pot roast, sausage and others, can be parboiled before grilling to reduce the fat content.

- When shopping for red meats, buy the leanest cuts you can find. Fat will show up as an opaque white coating, or can also run through the meat fibers, as marbling. Although most of the fat (the white coating) can be trimmed away, there isn't much that can be done about the marbling. Stay away from well marbled cuts of meat.

- Home from work late with no time for marinating meat? Pound meat lightly with a mallet or rolling pin, pierce with a fork, sprinkle lightly with meat tenderizer and add marinade. Refrigerate for about 20 minutes and you'll have succulent, tender meat.

- Marinating is a cinch if you use a plastic bag. The meat stays in the marinade and it's easy to turn and rearrange. Cleanup is easy; just toss the bag.

- It's easier to thinly slice meat if it's partially frozen.

- Tomatoes added to roasts will help to naturally tenderize them. Tomatoes contain an acid that works well to break down meats.

- Whenever possible, cut meats across the grain; they will be easier to eat and have a better appearance.

- When frying meat, sprinkle paprika over it to turn it golden brown.

- Thaw all meats in the refrigerator for maximum safety.

- Refrigerate poultry promptly after purchasing. Keep it in the coldest section of your refrigerator for up to two days. Freeze poultry for longer storage. Never leave poultry at room temperature for more than two hours.

- If you're microwaving skinned chicken, cover the baking dish with vented clear plastic wrap to keep the chicken moist.

- Lemon juice rubbed on fish before cooking will enhance the flavor and help maintain a good color.

- Scaling a fish is easier if vinegar is rubbed on the scales first.

Meat, Poultry & Seafood

BARBEQUED PORK TENDERLOIN

Barbara Grossman

2 (about 1½-lb.) pork
  tenderloins
1 c. light corn syrup
½ c. light soy sauce
½ c. ketchup

4 T. Worcestershire sauce
4 T. cider vinegar
2 tsp. dry mustard
2 cloves garlic, crushed

Mix in medium bowl, corn syrup, light soy sauce, ketchup, Worcestershire sauce, cider vinegar, dry mustard and garlic. Whisk until smooth. Place pork tenderloin in Ziploc bag with marinade and seal. Chill in refrigerator 8 hours or overnight, turning occasionally. Remove meat from marinade and grill for 25 to 30 minutes on medium-high heat, turning. Meanwhile, boil marinade 5 minutes and serve as a gravy over pork.

BBQ PORK TENDERLOIN

Leslie McQueen

1½ to 2-lb. pork tenderloin
1 c. soy sauce

⅓ c. sesame oil
1 T. ginger

Marinate 3 hours in refrigerator. Place on grill. Turn every 15 minutes and baste with marinade. Approximate cooking time: 2 hours.

PORK MEDALLIONS WITH APRICOT GLAZE

Michelle James

1½ pork tenderloins (about 1
  lb.)
Salt & freshly ground pepper to
  taste

1 sm. garlic clove
2 T. vegetable oil
¼ c. port
2 T. apricot jam

Cut the pork tenderloins into 8 medallions about ¼ inch thick. Season with salt and pepper. Mince the garlic. Heat the oil in a large frying pan over high heat. When the oil is hot, add the pork medallions and cook, turning once, until the pork is nicely browned outside with not trace of pink in the center, about 6 minutes total cooking time. Remove the pork to a platter. Add the garlic to the pan and cook, stirring, for 30 seconds. Whisk in the port and apricot jam and boil over high heat, stirring, another minute or so. Return the pork and any accumulated juices to the pan and heat through. Serve immediately.

ORANGE STUFFED PORK CHOPS

Lorraine Mondulick

1 c. soft bread crumbs
¼ c. raisins
1 T. finely chopped onion
1 T. sugar
1 tsp. salt
¼ tsp. crushed rosemary

1 T. oil
2 T. butter, melted
1 T. grated orange rind
¼ c. orange juice
6 pork chops, 1-2 inches thick

Combine: bread, raisins, onions, sugar, 1 teaspoon salt, rosemary, butter, orange rind and orange juice in bowl. Mix well. Cut a packet along the fat side of each chop, cutting almost to the bone. Stuff each chop with stuffing. Secure with toothpicks. Brown chops on both sides in oil in large skillet. Season with salt and pepper. Place in baking pan. Cover and bake 325° for 45 to 60 minutes. Uncover and bake 45 to 60 minutes longer.

CONNECTICUT YANKEE SPARE RIBS

Joe Cueto

6 lbs. spareribs, cut into 3 rib
  pieces
1½ tsp. salt
1 tsp. garlic salt
1 tsp. onion salt
1 lemon, thinly sliced

½ c. catsup
¼ c. mustard
¼ c. vinegar
2 T. Worcestershire sauce
1 tsp. chili powder

Place spare ribs in shallow pan, meat side up. Sprinkle with salts. Top with lemon slices. Cover with cover or tin foil. Bake at 350° for 1 hour. Remove fat, refrigerate ribs until grilling time. Combine catsup, mustard, vinegar, Worcestershire sauce and chili powder in a bowl. Brush ribs with sauce. Place ribs on 6 to 8 inches above hot coals. Grill 30 minutes, turning and basting frequently.

PORK CHOPS AND RICE

Jan Winn

6 pork chops
1½ cans beef consomme
³/₈ c. water (little less than ½ c.)
1 or 2 onion slices for the top of
  each chop

10-12 sliced green olives
3 T. olive juice
1 c. uncooked rice

Salt and pepper chops and brown. Place in greased 9 x 13-inch pan. Put onion slices on top of chops. Pour the rice into gaps around the chops. Mix consomme, water and olive juice; pour over the rice. Scatter olives slices over all. Sprinkle with paprika. Cover tightly with foil and bake 1½ hours at 350°.

34808-00

LINGUINE WITH PORK AND CURRY

Martha Swift

8 oz. linguine
1 T. vegetable oil
½ lb. pork tenderloin, sliced
  thin
1 red or green pepper, sliced
  thin
1 onion, coarsely chopped

2 tsp. curry powder
1 c. chicken broth
10 oz. frozen peas & carrots,
  thawed
¼ c. mango chutney
1 tsp. cornstarch mixed with 1
  T. water

Cook linguine until tender. Drain. Heat 2 teaspoons oil over medium heat until hot. Add pork stirring until pork is cooked. Transfer pork to plate. Add remaining onion to skillet. Add pepper and onion, stir until crisp-tender. Stir in curry powder. Cook 30 seconds. Stir in broth, peas, carrots, chutney and cornstarch mix. Return pork to skillet, stirring and cooking until mixture thickens and peas and carrots are warm. Put mixture in bowl, add linguine, toss to mix.

MARINATED GRILLED LAMB

June Zuranski

1 c. olive oil
⅔ c. lemon juice
3 cloves garlic, crushed
2 bay leaves
6 sprigs parsley, chopped

½ tsp. pepper
2 tsp. salt
1 T. each sage, thyme &
  rosemary

Butterfly a boneless leg of lamb. Remove all fat if possible Mix oil, lemon juice, garlic, bay leaves, salt, pepper and ½ tablespoon of herbs. Marinate lamb 24 hours in this mixture, turning several times in refrigerator.

Sauce:

½ c. beef stock
¼ c. red wine
2 T. butter or margarine

3 T. chopped parsley
Add rest of herbs

After marinating 24 hours, drain meat. Reserve marinade. Sear meat on grill high on each side.

PARTY LAMB SHANKS

Helen Cueto

6 lamb shanks
1 clove garlic, thinly sliced
1 tsp. salt
¼ tsp. pepper
2 T. cooking oil
4-oz. can mushrooms
½ c. chopped onions

1 c. white cooking wine
2 T. flour
½ c. water
½ tsp. dill seed
1 tsp. paprika
1 c. sour cream

Make a slit to bone in each shank. Insert a sliver of garlic in each. Sprinkle with salt and pepper. Brown on all sides in oil in large skillet or Dutch oven. Add mushrooms with liquid, onion and wine. Cover. Simmer 1½ hours, until meat is tender. Remove shanks to heated platter. Combine flour and water. Stir into drippings. Cook, stirring constantly, until mixture thickens. Reduce heat. Stir in dill seed, paprika and sour cream. Heat, but do not boil. Serve sauce over shanks.

VEAL MARSALA

Rhonda Maule

4 lg. slices veal cutlet
¼ c. flour
½ tsp. salt
¼ tsp. pepper
½ tsp. dried oregano

4 T. oil
4 T. butter
1 c. fresh sliced mushrooms
½ c. Marsala wine

Pound cutlets ¼-inch thick. Combine flour, salt, pepper and oregano; dredge veal cutlets in flour mixture; shake off excess. Heat oil and butter in large nonstick skillet over medium heat until bubbles. Cook in skillet until lightly browned on first side. Turn over; add mushrooms. Cook about 2 minutes or lightly browned, stirring mushrooms so they cook evenly. Add Marsala to skillet. Cover pan, turn heat to low; simmer 10 minutes. Serve immediately, pouring pan juices over meat.

VEAL SCALLOPINI

Marie Scott

1½ lbs. veal round steak, cut
  ½-inch thick
¼ c. all-purpose flour
½ tsp. salt
⅛ tsp. pepper
¼ c. butter
1 c. sliced fresh mushrooms
¼ c. sherry

¼ c. water
2 T. minced chives
2 T. minced parsley
1 T. lemon juice
⅛ tsp. rosemary
⅛ tsp. tarragon
⅛ tsp. marjoram

(continued)

34808-00

Cut steak into 6 pieces. Combine flour, salt, pepper; coat meat with seasoned flour. Pound meat with meat hammer or edge of a heavy saucer until ¼-inch thick, sprinkling meat with flour mixture as needed. Fry in butter in skillet until well browned on both sides. Remove to heated platter. Sauté mushrooms in skillet until tender. Add sherry, water, lemon juice, chives, parsley, rosemary, tarragon and marjoram. Heat and pour sauce over meat.

MARINATED FLANK STEAK

Gail Fouraker

2 (1-to 1¼-lb.) flank steaks
½ c. vegetable oil
¼ c. teriyaki sauce
1 T. minced onion

3 T. honey
½ tsp. garlic powder
½ tsp. ground ginger

Prick both sides of steak with fork and place in a large shallow dish. Combine oil, sauce, onion, honey, garlic powder and ginger. Pour over steaks. Cover; marinate 24 hours in refrigerator, turning occasionally. Remove steaks from marinade. Grill over hot coals 4 to 5 minutes on each side or until desired doneness. **To serve:** Slice cross-grain into thin slices. Yield: 6 to 8 servings.

BEEF OVER RICE OR NOODLES

Doris Coones

3-4 lbs. stew beef, uncooked &
  lean
2 pkgs. Lipton onion soup mix

2 cans mushroom soup
1 c. water
½ c. white wine

Mix, beef, onion and mushroom soup, water and wine. Place in large casserole. Cover and bake in a 325° oven for 3 hours. Serve over cooked rice or noodles.

CHICKEN IN WINE SAUCE

Janet Schenone

Chicken pieces
1 can cream of mushroom soup
½ c. wine OR ⅓ c. lemon juice
Flour

Salt
Pepper
Garlic powder
Onion flakes

Salt and pepper chicken and coat with flour. Fry chicken pieces in small amount of oil and set aside. Add soup and wine or lemon juice to pan drippings. Add ½ cup water and season to taste with garlic powder and onion flakes. Heat soup mixture until bubbly. Place chicken in baking dish and pour soup mixture on top. Bake 1 to 1½ hours at 300°. Serve with rice, pasta or mashed potatoes.

CHICKEN WITH SUN-DRIED TOMATOES

Annette Gregorio

2 lbs. boneless chicken breasts
3 oz. melted butter
3 oz. olive oil
2 T. chopped shallots
2 T. chopped garlic

4 oz. sun-dried tomatoes
6 oz. cream sherry
10 oz. chicken broth
Sm. amount flour to coat
   chicken

Dredge chicken in flour and sauté in oil and butter until golden brown. Remove chicken and add shallots, garlic and dried tomatoes to pan. Sauté for about 3 minutes. Add sherry and reduce. Add chicken broth and simmer for a few minutes. Pour over chicken and serve over rice or angel hair pasta.

CHICKEN CORDON BLEU

Lorraine Mondulick

2 sheets frozen puff pastry
8 pieces boned & skinned
  chicken breast
3 T. butter

8 slices Swiss cheese
8 slices ham
Salt
Pepper

Thaw pastry sheets about 20 minutes. Meanwhile, season chicken breasts with salt and pepper. Sauté in butter about 1 minute on each side. Drain, set aside to cool. Unfold thawed pastry sheets. Cut pastry into 4 quarters. On a lightly floured board, roll out each pastry square large enough to enclose chicken breast. Place chicken in center of each pastry square. Top with cheese and ham slice. Wrap pastry around chicken with hand and cheese. Pinch edges to seal. Place on ungreased baking sheet. Bake at 350° for 20 minutes. Makes 8 servings.

CHICKEN DIVAN

Martha Swift

1 pkg. Stove Top stuffing
1/4 c. margarine
1 2/3 c. hot water
6 chicken breast halves

1 1/3 c. broccoli cuts, thawed
1 (12 oz.) chicken gravy
1 (2.5 oz.) mushrooms
1-2 T. apple juice or white wine

Place contents of vegetable/seasoning packet and 2 tablespoons margarine in large bowl. Add hot water, stir to partially melt margarine. Add stuffing crumbs, stir to moisten. Let stand until water if absorbed. Meanwhile, cook and stir chicken in remaining margarine until lightly browned about 5 minutes. Place chicken in baking dish. Top each piece with stuffing and broccoli. Mix gravy, mushrooms and juice; pour over broccoli and stuffing. Cover and bake at 350° for 30 minutes.

68

34808-00

CHICKEN TARRAGON

Pauline H. Vachan

2 lg. whole chicken breasts,
  boneless, skinless, split into 4
  pieces
12 saltines, crushed fine
1/4 tsp. tarragon
1/2 tsp. salt

1/4 tsp. pepper
1/2 c. white wine
1/4 c. margarine or butter
1 c. sliced mushrooms
1/2 c. chicken broth
1 c. white or red grapes

Wet chicken, shake excess water off. Roll in saltines, tarragon and salt and pepper mixed together first. Let set for 15 minutes. Sauté chicken in margarine until lightly browned. Remove from heat and place in oblong baking dish in single layer. In meantime, sauté onion and mushrooms for 2 to 3 inches, add chicken broth and white wine. Bring to a boil, then pour over chicken. Bake uncovered at 350° for 35 minutes, then sprinkle grapes (cut in half) on top. Bake an additional 10 to 15 minutes more.

CHICKEN SUZANNE

Joan Racelis

4-6 half chicken breasts
Salt & pepper
1 stick margarine
1/2 c. sour cream

1/2 c. sherry
1 (10³/₄-oz.) can condensed
  cream of mushroom soup

Season chicken with salt and pepper. Brown in melted margarine. Remove to greased shallow casserole. Add sour cream, sherry and mushroom soup to melted margarine. Mix well and pour over chicken. Cover and bake at 350° for 1½ hours. Makes 4 to 6 servings.

CHICKEN BREASTS IN SOUR CREAM ALMOND SAUCE

Lyn Griffiths

6 boneless, skinless chicken
  breasts, halved
3 T. butter
2 T. chopped onion
1 clove garlic, minced
1 T. tomato paste
2 T. flour

1½ c. chicken stock
3 T. dry sherry
2 T. chopped almonds
1/2 tsp. tarragon
Salt & pepper
3/4 c. sour cream
1/2 c. grated Gruyere cheese

Sauté chicken in butter on both sides. Remove from pan. Add onion and garlic. Stir for 2 to 3 minutes. Add tomato paste and flour; stir until blended. Gradually add chicken stock and sherry. Stir until blended. Return chicken, almonds, tarragon, salt and pepper. Cover and simmer for 30 minutes. Arrange chicken in ovenproof serving dish. Stir sour cream into sauce and pour over chicken. Sprinkle with cheese and brown under broiler.

CHICKEN GORILLA

Jocelyn Stevens

1 pkg. boneless, skinless
  chicken breasts
2 cans tomato soup
1 can stewed tomatoes
1 T. sour cream
1 box instant rice

1 red pepper & green pepper
1 sm. onion
Crushed red pepper
Basil
Oregano
Cooking oil

Poach chicken in microwave. Cook completely. Cut up chicken in small pieces. Set aside. Cut up onion (into rings) and peppers. In large deep pan, put silver dollar-size cooking oil. Add onions. Cook until clear. Add cut-up peppers. Add 2 cans soup and can stewed tomatoes with juice. Lower heat and add pepper, basil and oregano to taste. Simmer 20 minutes. Put in chicken breast pieces. Simmer 20 minutes. Cook rice as directed on box. Taste chicken, sauce and add spices, if needed. The longer you simmer chicken, sauce the more tender. Right before serving, add sour cream to chicken and sauce and stir. Your sauce is now orange. Put rice in big bowl. Pour chicken and sauce over rice. Serve with rolls.

DIJON BAKED CHICKEN

Shirley Grube

½ c. dry white wine
½ c. chicken broth
2 T. Dijon mustard
2 T. coarse ground mustard

1⅓ c. bread crumbs
2 T. Parmesan cheese
⅓ c. chopped parsley
12 (4-oz.) chicken breasts

Mix wine, broth and mustard in small bowl. Mix bread crumbs, cheese and parsley in small bowl. Coat chicken with wine mixture, then dip in bread crumbs. Place chicken on pan sprayed with Pam. Bake in 475° oven for 15 to 20 minutes or until lightly browned and tender.

WALNUT CHICKEN BREAST WITH MUSTARD-SOUR CREAM SAUCE

Michelle James

4 skinless chicken breast
  halves, trimmed (about 1 lb.)
Salt & pepper to taste
4-5 T. olive oil
3 T. Dijon-style mustard

½ c. (2½ oz.) finely chopped
  walnuts
⅔ c. sour cream, regular or
  reduced-fat

Season each chicken breast lightly with salt and pepper place them between sheets of plastic wrap. Pound to a uniform thickness of about 1 inch. Set aside. Mix 2 tablespoons of the olive oil with 2 tablespoons of the mustard and brush the chicken breasts with this mixture. Place

(continued)

34808-00

the walnuts on a plate. Coat both sides of the chicken with the chopped walnuts, pressing gently to help them adhere. Set the breast on a rack for 10 minutes. Heat 2 tablespoons of the remaining oil in a 10-inch skillet over medium-high heat. Add the chicken breasts and sauté on other sides, for 2 to 3 minutes per side, until the nuts are deep brown and the chicken meat feels firm to the touch. Add more oil, if needed. When the chicken is done, remove pieces to a platter and keep warm. Remove the pan from the heat, discard any burned nuts and stir the sour cream and remaining tablespoon mustard into the hot pan drippings. If needed, heat through over low heat. Serve each portion of chicken in a pool of sauce.

CHICKEN MARSALA

Janet Barry

4 boneless chicken breasts	2 sticks butter
1 c. Marsala wine	½ c. flour
Salt & pepper	8 oz. fresh mushrooms

Wash and dry thoroughly chicken breast. In a zippered plastic bag add flour, salt and pepper. Take 2 chicken breasts at a time and shake in the bag. Melt 1 stick of butter in a frying pan. Add chicken breast and cook 5 minutes on each side or longer until cooked. Meanwhile, melt 1 stick butter. Add cooked chicken, mushrooms on sides. Pour 1 cup Marsala wine over chicken and mushrooms. Set burner to medium to low and cook another 10 to 20 minutes or longer. You don't want it to burn. Gravy will thicken as it cooks. Serves 4.

IRRESISTIBLE CHICKEN

Leslie McQueen

1 (2½-to 3½-lb.) chicken, cut into parts	1¼ c. Italian-seasoned bread crumbs
½ c. Hellmann's real mayonnaise	

Brush chicken on all sides with mayonnaise. Place bread crumbs in large plastic food bag. Add chicken one piece at a time; shake to coat well. Place on rack in broiler pan. Bake in 425° oven for about 40 minutes or until golden brown and tender.

EASY TANGY CHICKEN

Jocelyn Stevens
Diane Neal

8 oz. Catalina salad dressing	1 env. dry onion soup mix
½ c. peach preserves or 1 can cranberry sauce (with berries)	8 boneless, skinless, chicken breasts

(continued)

Combine salad dressing, preserves and soup mix. Place chicken in ungreased baking dish. Pour dressing mixture over chicken. Cover and bake at 350° for 20 minutes; baste. Bake, uncovered, 20 minutes longer or until chicken is done. Make 8 servings.

GRILLED CHICKEN BURGERS

Laura Mondulick

1 lb. ground skinless, boneless
  chicken or turkey
½ c. plain dry greased crumbs
2 green onions, chopped

1 T. lemon juice
2 tsp. Worcestershire sauce
¼ tsp. salt
2 T. barbecue sauce

Combine all ingredients. Use hands to mix thoroughly. Make six patties. Grill 4 to 6 minutes per side or until no longer pink.

CHICKEN FAJITAS

Martha Swift

4 boneless chicken breast
  halves, cut into thin strips
¾ c. Italian dressing
1 sm. onion, sliced
1 sm. green pepper, sliced

1 sm. red pepper, sliced
1 sm. yellow pepper, sliced
1 c. sliced fresh mushrooms
½ tsp. garlic salt
2 T. lemon juice

In heavy plastic bag combine chicken strips, dressing and refrigerate for several hours or overnight turning bag occasionally. Drain. Heat a 12-inch nonstick skillet over medium-high heat. Stir-fry chicken strips and onions for 2 minutes. Add pepper strips and mushrooms, cook and stir until chicken is done and peppers are tender-crisp. Season with garlic salt, lemon, salt and pepper. Serve in warm tortillas. Top with picante sauce and sour cream.

LIZ'S EVERGLADES SHRIMP DINNER

Marti Smith

⅓-½ can Old Bay seasoning
12-18 sm. new potatoes, fresh,
  unpeeled
6-8 corn ears on the cob,
  broken in half
Approximately 3 lbs. or 3 lg.
  links kielbasa sausage
  (smoked), cut into bite-size
  pieces

Everglades seasoning, enough
  to season all ingredients
32-36 FRESH shrimp, VERY LG.
  of jumbo "heads off", unpeeled
Butter & shrimp sauce or
  cocktail sauce or BOTH

In a extra large pan or Dutch oven, put enough water to fill ½ to ⅔ full; add Old Bay seasonings. Add clean, unpeeled, small potatoes.

(continued)

34808-00

Bring to a boil for about 4 minutes or until they just **begin** to get soft. Add cut up sausage, continuing to boil about 4 to 5 minutes, then add corn. Boil all of this together for about 4 more minutes, then add shrimp. Continue to boil until shrimp begins or does turn **pink**. When shrimp is done, remove all ingredients from water and drain in colander. Take each ingredients and shake on the **Everglades** seasoning.

SEAFOOD STEW WITH BASIL AND TOMATOES

Barbara Grossman

¼ c. olive oil
1¼ c. chopped onion
2 T. chopped garlic
4 tsp. dried oregano
1½ tsp. fennel seeds
2½ c. crushed tomatoes with purée
2½ c. bottled clam juice

1 c. dry white wine
2 (6½-oz.) cans chopped clams, drained & reserve juice
1 lb. uncooked lg. shrimp, peeled & deveined
1 (6-oz.) can crabmeat, drained
½ c. chopped fresh basil
Cayenne to taste

Heat olive oil in heavy large pot over medium heat. Add onion, garlic, oregano and fennel seed. Sauté until onion is tender, about 8 minutes. Add tomatoes, clam juice, white wine and juice reserved from calms. Increase heat and boil until slightly thickened about 20 minutes. (Can be made up to this point ahead of time. Bring to simmer before proceeding.) Add clams, shrimp and crabmeat. Decrease heat to simmer for 2 minutes. Mix in fresh basil and simmer until shrimp are just opaque in center, about 2 minutes. Season to taste with cayenne, salt and pepper. Serve in large bowls with a crusty bread or over your favorite pasta! Serves 4.

SALMON EN PAPILLOTE WITH SPINACH

Louise Fisher

4 sun dried tomatoes
10-oz. bag fresh spinach
Dried tarragon
4⅓ lb. skinless salmon fillets
1 tsp. extra-virgin olive oil

½ tsp. balsamic vinegar
Salt
Freshly ground pepper
2 c. cooked rice

Preheat oven to 400°. Soak 4 sun-dried tomatoes in hot water to cover 30 minutes. Meanwhile, thoroughly wash a 10-ounce bag of fresh spinach. Transfer spinach, undrained to a large pot and cook over medium heat until it is completely wilted, letting the water that clings to the leaves steam the spinach. Drain, coarsely chop and divide it into four portions; set aside. Drain tomatoes, cut them into slivers and divide into four portions; set aside. Tear 4 sheets of aluminum foil, each slightly longer than a foot. On one sheet, layer half a portion of sun-dried tomato, half a portion of spinach, a pinch of dried tarragon, one (⅓-pound) skinless salmon fillet, the other half of the sun-dried tomato and spinach and

(continued)

another pinch of tarragon. Drizzle with 1 teaspoon extra-virgin olive oil and ½ teaspoon balsamic vinegar and season with salt and freshly ground black pepper. Bring the sides of the foil up to meet each other, crimp them together to close the package but leaving as much air inside as possible. Repeat this process for three more fillets. Place the packets on a cooked sheet or baking pan bake 15 minutes. Pierce the package carefully with a knife to release steam before opening. Serve each portion with ¼ cup cooked rice. Makes 4 servings.

SALMON WITH RASPBERRY SAUCE

Lillian Treiser

½ c. orange juice
⅓ c. chopped green onions
1½ T. brown sugar
1½ T. low sodium soy sauce
1 T. white wine vinegar
¼ tsp. salt

¼ tsp. pepper
1½ lbs. salmon fillet (about 1 inch thick)
Cooking spray
1 c. raspberries, frozen

Combine juice, onions, sugar, soy sauce, vinegar, salt and pepper in Ziploc plastic bag; seal and marinate in refrigerator 20 minutes, turning bag occasionally. Remove salmon from bag. Reserve marinade. Place salmon skin side down on baking sheet, sprayed with cooking spray. Broil 12 minutes or until fish flakes easily when tested with fork. Pour reserved marinade into small skillet and bring to boil, gently stir in raspberries. Cut salmon into four equal portion and spoon raspberry sauce over salmon. Make 4 servings.

SALMON STEAKS WITH HONEY MUSTARD GLAZE

Fran Fitzpatrick

1 T. orange juice
1 tsp. dry mustard
1 tsp. safflower oil

2 T. honey
4 salmon steaks (about 1¼ lbs.)

In a small saucepan, combine orange juice and mustard, stirring to dissolve mustard. Stir in oil and honey; heat over low heat until glaze is well combined. Brush both sides of steak with Honey-Mustard Glaze, place on a large, shallow baking pan or dish and bake in a 400° oven for 10 to 15 minutes. Serve piping hot. Makes 4 servings.

34808-00

SALMON MELT SUPREME

Leslie McQueen

2 (6-oz.) cans skinless,
  boneless, salmon
¼ c. (lite) mayonnaise
1 T. minced red onion
1 tsp. lemon juice
¼ tsp. Dijon mustard

⅛ tsp. black pepper
4 English muffins, split &
  toasted
2 oz. grated part-skim
  mozzarella cheese
¼ c. grated carrot (opt.)

Drain salmon well. Combine salmon, mayonnaise, onion, lemon juice, Dijon mustard and black pepper. Mix well. Spread mixture on toasted muffin halves. Top with cheese. Place muffins on microwave-proof plate. Microwave on **high** until cheese is melted (about 25 to 45 seconds). Top with grated carrot. Serve hot.

PORCHED FISH SUPREME

Gerald Wixson

4 firm white (8-oz.) fish fillets
  (such as walleye or grouper)
1 (14½-oz.) can stewed
  tomatoes, drained
1 med. white onion, sliced
1 green pepper, cored & sliced
  in rings

1 lemon, sliced
2 tsp. oregano
Salt, if desired
¼ tsp. coarsely ground black
  pepper
Olive nonstick spray

Lay a 24-inch length of 18-inch wide heavy-duty aluminum foil on a flat surface. Spray an area approximately 12 x 18 inches with nonstick spray. Place the fish fillets side by side in a single layer. Spread the drained stewed tomatoes, onion slices, green pepper rings, lemon slices, oregano, salt and pepper evenly over the fillets. Cover with an aluminum foil sheet of equal size. Fold all edges lightly several times to prevent the escape of juices and steam. Slide unto a cookie sheet carefully to prevent tearing for each transport. Slice into a grate over the hot coals on an open fire, on a barbecue at medium-low heat or in an oven at 400°. Cook until foil puffs up full. Poke two small holes in the top foil to allow steam out and cook for 10 minutes more (15 minutes for thicker grouper fillets). Split the foil open (have your camera ready) and serve with boiled new potatoes. Serves four.

STUFFED FLOUNDER BEARNAISE

Martl Smith

6 fresh founder fillets or as
  many as needed
Crab meat or imitation crab
  meat in chunks
Cracker crumbs

1 egg
1-2 T. milk
Chopped onion & celery
Salt & pepper to taste
Knorr Bearnaise sauce

(continued)

Heat oven to 350°. In a bowl: Crumble plenty of crab meat, add cracker crumbs, egg, milk, onion, celery and seasoning. Mix together, as you would stuffing for turkey. Keep mixture moist. If it is too dry, add more milk or another egg. (Make enough to almost cover the tops of the fish.) Each piece of fish will need mound of the stuffing on top. Set this aside. Use a shallow baking dish or cookie sheet with sides. Melt enough butter to "grease" the bottom of the baking dish. Lay the fish on the dish and a put a "dot" of butter on each piece. (You can put a little salt and pepper on fish, if desired.) Bake the fish covered with foil for approximately 3 to 5 minutes. Take fish from oven and put a "hump" of stuffing on each piece. (Enough to almost cover the top.) Make up 1 or 2 package of **Knorr Bearnaise Sauce** as the package instructs, but use a little more milk to thin the sauce a little. Spoon enough sauce on each piece of fish to cover it and pour enough **around** the fish to cover the bottom of the baking dish. (Put the rest aside.) Cover this with foil and bake approximately 20 to 30 minutes. (Just long enough to bake stuffing and make fish white and flaky.) You may want to spoon a little more sauce on about half way through baking time. **Do not overbake.** When just about done, remove foil, so each piece will "brown".

SOLE FLORTENTINE
(Microwave)

Marcie Lynn Leffent

2 (10-oz.) pkgs. frozen chopped spinach
1 T. dry minced onion
$1/2$ tsp. grated lemon peel
$1/2$ tsp. salt
$1/4$ tsp. pepper

$1/2$ tsp. dry mustard
2 T. grated Parmesan cheese
1 tsp. parsley flakes
$1/2$ tsp. paprika
1 lb. sole fillets

Place spinach packages in microwave oven on high for 6 to $6^1/2$ minutes. Drain well. Place in 8 x 8-inch baking dish. Stir in onion, lemon peel, salt, pepper, dry mustard. Spread spinach mixture over bottom of baking dish. Combine Parmesan cheese, parsley and paprika. Set aside. Place fish on top of mixture. Cover. Microwave on high 4 minutes. Rearrange. Sprinkle with Parmesan cheese mixture. Cover. Microwave on high for 2 to 6 minutes or until fish flakes with fork. Serves 4.

TUNA CAKES

Marie Marshall

$1/4$ c. bread crumbs
1 (12-oz.) can white tuna
$3/4$ c. shredded cheddar cheese
$1/2$ c. mayonnaise
1 egg, lightly beaten

$1/3$ c. Ranch dressing
$1/2$ c. finely chopped green pepper
2 T. vegetable oil

(continued)

34808-00

In large bowl, combine bread crumbs, tuna, cheddar cheese, mayonnaise, egg and green pepper. Shape mixture into patties. Heat oil in skillet over medium heat. Cook patties 3 to 4 minutes on each side. Serves 4 to 6 people.

TUNA MELT

Leslie McQueen

1 (12-oz.) can solid white albacore tuna, drained & flaked
½ c. light mayonnaise
1½ T. sweet pickle relish
1½ T. chopped onion
½ T. mustard

3 English muffins, split & toasted
6 tomato slices, halved
6 slices light cheddar or American cheese

In medium bowl, combine tuna, mayonnaise, pickle relish, onion and mustard; mix well. Spread about ⅓ cup on each muffin half. Top with tomato slices and a cheese slice. Broil 4 to 5 minutes or until cheese is melted.

MARYLAND CRAB CAKES

Lorraine McCullough

1 lb. crab meat
2 tsp. Worcestershire sauce
2 T. mustard
1 T. mayonnaise

6 crackers
1 egg
Old Bay seasoning

Remove shell from crabmeat and drain. Crush crackers. Mix crab meat, Worcestershire sauce, mustard, mayonnaise, crackers and egg in a bowl. Add Old Bay seasoning to taste (start with approximately ½ cup). Makes 8 to 12 crab cakes. Deep fry until golden brown or place in pan. Cover and broil for approximately 10 minutes. Remove cover; bake at 350° until golden brown.

CRAB CAKES

Mike Button

1 lb. lump crabmeat
1 tsp. Worcestershire sauce
1 T. mayonnaise/salad dressing
1 egg

Parsley
Salt & pepper
Old Bay seasoning
Butter

Combine all ingredients. Form into patties. Sauté in butter.

ORANGE ROUGHY WITH TRELAWNY SAUCE

Valerie Johnstone

Orange rough fillets or snapper
  (½ lb. per person)
3 T. fresh lemon juice
3 egg yolks

1 stick butter, cut in half (cold)
1 T. (approximately) garlic
  powder

Put yolks in small saucepan with lemon juice, beat together with fork until mixed and pasty. Place half the butter in pan, melt slowly over low heat, stirring constantly until melted. Add garlic to taste and second half butter stick, stir until melted and thickened. Place fillets on broiler pan. Broil until done. Spoon sauce over fillets and broil carefully until sauce bubbles and is slightly brown.

NANNY SNOW'S SEAFOOD SUPREME

Lorraine Mondulick

1½ lbs. sole (roll & secure with
  toothpick)
1 lb. sea scallops
1 lb. shrimp
1 lb. mushrooms
Sm. onion
2-3 stalks celery & leaves

2 c. water
1 bay leaf
Salt & pepper
2 T. butter
4 T. flour
1 c. light cream
1 can crabmeat

Bring water, onion, celery, bay leaf, salt and pepper to a boil. Simmer and poach sole. Remove sole and poach scallops. Remove scallops and poach shrimp. Reserve 1 cup of poaching water. Cook mushrooms in butter and drain. Take toothpicks carefully out of sole and put all fish and mushrooms in a casserole. Make a sauce with 4 tablespoons flour, 1 cup of reserved poaching water, 1 cup cream and 1 can crabmeat. Pour over fish. Sprinkle with Parmesan cheese. Bake at 350° for 30 minutes.

SEA SCALLOPS WITH GARLIC AND SUN-DRIED TOMATOES

Michelle James

1½ lbs. cape scallops
Salt & freshly ground black
  pepper to taste
1 T. olive oil
1 T. finely chopped garlic

1 c. oil-packed sun-dried
  tomatoes, drained & julienned
Juice of ½ lemon
2 T. unsalted butter
3 T. chopped Italian parsley

Pick through scallions, removing straps and any particles of shell. Place the scallops in a colander to drain so they are as dry as possible. Prepare, measure and have all the other ingredients ready to go. Heat a sauté pan until smoking hot. (Use two pans if necessary to prevent overcrowding.) Season the scallops with salt and pepper. Add the oil

(continued)

34808-00

and the scallops to the pan, leaving little space for the garlic. As soon as the scallops hit the pan, add the garlic. Do not move the pan or stir the scallops. After 30 seconds, add the sun-dried tomatoes and toss. Cook for 30 seconds more. Add the lemon juice, butter and parsley. Remove from heat and toss or stir until butter melts. Check seasonings and serve immediately.

OUT-OF-THIS-WORLD SHRIMP

Susan Moore

1½ lbs. cooked shrimp
2 T. butter
⅛ tsp. white pepper
½ tsp. salt
1¼ c. milk, warm to hot
3 T. sherry

1 (14-oz.) can artichoke hearts, washed & drained
1 (16-oz.) can colossal mushrooms or 1 lb. fresh
⅛ tsp. paprika
4 T. grated Parmesan cheese

Melt butter. Add flour and blend with a wire whisk. Slowly stir in heated milk. Add salt and pepper. Cook and stir until sauce is smooth and boiling. Remove from heat and add sherry. Place artichoke hearts in a large buttered casserole dish. Scatter the shrimp and mushrooms over the hearts. Cover with white sauce and sprinkle generously with paprika and Parmesan cheese. Bake in preheated 350° oven for 30 minutes. Serves 6.

BROILED GARLIC SHRIMP

Leslie McQueen

1 lb. jumbo shrimp, peeled & cleaned
½ c. bread crumbs

All Natural Pam garlic flavor seasoning spray

Preheat broiler. Spray each shrimp with Pam seasonings spray about **1 second**. Coat with bread crumbs. Spread again with Pam for **1 second**. Place shrimp on broiler pan or baking sheets. Broil 8 to 10 minutes or until done. Serve over rice or pasta. Makes 4 servings.

BEER BOILED SHRIMP

Mildred Gregory

2 lbs. shrimp in shells
2 cans beer, any kind
1 or 2 sm. cloves garlic, pressed
1 bay leaf
1 onion, quartered

1 tsp. red pepper
1 piece celery
1 lemon, quartered
2-3 T. salt
Enough water to cover shrimp

Combine all ingredients, except shrimp in large pot. Bring to a rolling boil. Add shrimp to the boiling mixture. Add hot water if the liquid doesn't

(continued)

cover shrimp. Quickly return to a boil. After boiling again, cover and cook 5 minutes. At end of cooking, remove from heat and allow to stand covered in the water for 10 minutes. Drain shrimp well. Place a few ice cubes on cooked shrimp to cool quickly.

GRILLED LEMON PRAWNS

Barbara Grossman

1 c. olive oil
1 T. dried oregano, crumbled
1 T. dried thyme, crumbled
2 tsp. grated lemon zest
2 tsp. coarse salt

2 tsp. fresh ground pepper
24 prawns or jumbo shrimp
3 T. fresh lemon juice
Lemon wedges as
   accompaniment

In large bowl stir together (the oil, herbs, zest, salt and pepper. Add prawns or shrimp (peeled deveined) and toss to coat well. Let marinate, covered and chilled, for at least one hour or overnight. Stir in the lemon juice, let the mixture stand at room temperature for 30 minutes, drain in fine sieve. (Marinade can be reserved brought to boiling for 5 minutes and used as sauce.) Grill or broil prawn 4 inches from heat 3 to 4 minutes each side. Divide among 8 plates and serve with lemon wedges.

SEAFOOD MARINARA WITH PASTA

Judith Grant

1 lb. spaghetti
2 tsp. oregano
2 T. olive oil
2 T. butter

3 cloves garlic
2 tomatoes
1/2 c. Parmesan cheese

Sauce:

1 c. white wine
Knorr Marinara sauce
1 lb. fish (any kind)
1/2 lb. each shrimp/crabmeat
1 onion

1 tomatoes
1/2 tsp. red pepper
1/4 tsp. pepper
1/2 tsp. salt

Cook spaghetti al dente, drain. Add olive oil butter and oregano to spaghetti. Mix. Add salt, pepper to taste. Marinate fish with onion, garlic and salt for 1 hour. Chop onion and garlic; sauté in olive oil (3 tablespoons) with butter, (1 tablespoon) until golden. Chop tomatoes and add to onion; sauté. Cut fish into large squares. Cook, then add shrimp and crab. Dissolve Knorr sauce in 1 cup milk and add to fish to thicken. Add flour, if necessary. Before serving, add 1 cup of white wine and Parmesan cheese.

34808-00

Breads & Rolls

Helpful Hints

- Over-ripe bananas can be peeled and frozen in a plastic container until it's time to bake bread or cake.

- When baking bread, a small dish of water in the oven will help keep the crust from getting too hard or brown.

- Use shortening, not margarine or oil, to grease pans, as margarine and oil absorb more readily into the dough or batter (especially bread).

- Use a metal ice tray divider to cut biscuits in a hurry. Press into the dough, and biscuits will separate at dividing lines when baked.

- To make self-rising flour, mix 4 cups flour, 2 teaspoons salt and 2 tablespoons baking powder, and store in a tightly covered container.

- Hot water kills yeast. One way to tell the correct temperature is to pour the water over your forearm. If you cannot feel either hot or cold, the temperature is just right.

- When in doubt, always sift flour before measuring.

- When baking in a glass pan, reduce the oven temperature by 25°.

- When baking bread, you get a finer texture if you use milk. Water makes a coarser bread.

- If your biscuits are dry it could be from too much handling, or the oven temperature may not have been hot enough.

- Nut breads are better if stored 24 hours before serving.

- To make bread crumbs, toast the heels of bread and chop in a blender or food processor.

- Cracked eggs should only be used in dishes that are thoroughly cooked; they may contain bacteria.

- The freshness of eggs can be tested by placing them in a large bowl of cold water; if they float, do not use them.

- For a quick, low-fat crunchy topping for muffins, sprinkle the tops with Grape-Nuts cereal before baking.

Breads & Rolls

GARLIC BREAD

Laura Mondulick

½ c. butter or margarine, melted   2 T. minced fresh parsley
3-4 garlic cloves, minced
1 (1-lb.) loaf French bread,
  halved lengthwise

In a small bowl, combine butter and garlic. Brush over cut sides of bread; sprinkle with parsley. Place, cut side up, on a baking sheet. Bake at 350° for 8 minutes. Broil 4 to 6 inches from heat for 2 minutes or until golden brown. Cut into 2-inch slices. Serve warm. Makes 8 servings.

LEMON BREAD

Marie Marshall

⅓ c. melted butter   1½ c. flour
1 c. sugar   1 tsp. baking powder
2 eggs   1 tsp. salt
¼ tsp. almond extract   ⅓ c. milk

Combine the butter, eggs and extract. Mix in sugar, flour, baking powder and salt. Add the milk. Bake in a greased bread pan at 350° for 1 hour. Can also be baked as muffins for 45 minutes. Five minutes before removing bread from oven, combine 3 tablespoons lemon juice and ¼ to ½ cup sugar in a small saucepan. Heat over low heat until sugar begins to melt. When the bread is done, spoon sauce over hot bread. Leave in pan for 10 minutes.

STRAWBERRY BREAD

L.W.R.

3 c. all-purpose flour   4 eggs, beaten
2 c. sugar   1¼ c. vegetable oil
1 tsp. baking soda   2½ c. (20 oz.) chopped
1 tsp. salt   strawberries
1 tsp. cinnamon

Combine flour, sugar, baking soda, salt and cinnamon. Mix well. Combine eggs, oil, strawberries and add to dry mixture. Mix thoroughly. Spoon into 2 greased and floured loaf pans. Bake at 350° for 1 hour.

EASY BANANA BREAD

Lorraine Mondulick

2 c. flour	2 eggs
1 tsp. baking soda	1 c. (2 med.) mashed bananas
½ tsp. salt	⅓ c. milk
½ c. butter	1 tsp. lemon or vinegar
1 c. sugar	½ c. chopped nuts

Preheat oven to 350°. Sift flour, baking soda and salt. Cream butter. Gradually add sugar, creaming well. Add eggs and bananas; blend. Combine milk and lemon juice. Add dry ingredients to banana mixture, alternating with milk; begin and end with dry ingredients. Stir in nuts. Grease bottom of 9 x 5 x 3-inch pan. Pour in batter. Bake 60 to 70 minutes. Remove and cool on wire racks. Makes 1 loaf.

PUMPKIN BREAD

Ginny Orenstein

3⅓ c. flour	½ tsp. cinnamon
3 c. sugar	⅔ c. melted shortening
½ tsp. baking powder	⅔ c. water
2 tsp. soda	1 c. chopped pecans
2 tsp. salt	2 c. pumpkin
1 tsp. cloves	4 eggs

Sift together flour, sugar, baking powder, soda, salt, cinnamon and cloves. Stir in shortening, eggs, water, pecans and pumpkin. Pour into 2 large or 4 small loaf pans, greased and floured. Bake at 350° for 1 hour.

SWEET POTATO BREAD

Michelle James

1 pkg. dry yeast	1 tsp. salt
3 T. sugar	¾ lb. mashed, cooked sweet
2 eggs	potatoes
⅓ c. milk	3-4 c. flour
¼ c. warm water	1 stick melted, cooled butter

In small bowl, dissolve 1 tablespoon sugar in ¼ cup warm water. Add yeast let "proof" 25 minutes. In large bowl whisk eggs, milk, melted butter, sweet potatoes. Add yeast mixture, then remaining sugar, salt and 3 cups flour. Turn onto board and knead is as much of the 4th cup of flour as possible. Return to large cleaned bowl, which should be coated with melted butter. Cover with plastic wrap and let rise in warm area that is draft free. Dough should double in size in 2 to 4 hours. Punch down and shape into Parker House roll-size or stick-size rolls. Let rise again, should take 2 hours. Bake at 400° for 10 minutes.

34808-00

ZUCCHINI BREAD

Laura Mondulick

3 eggs
2 c. sugar
3 c. grated zucchini
1 c. oil
3 c. flour
2 tsp. vanilla

1 tsp. salt
1 tsp. cinnamon
1 tsp. baking powder
1 tsp. baking soda
1 c. chopped walnuts
½ c. chopped raisins

Mix eggs and sugar, add zucchini. Add oil and vanilla. Add flour, salt, cinnamon, baking soda, baking powder and mix well. Stir in nuts and raisins. Grease and flour 2 loaf pans. Bake at 350° for 60 to 70 minutes.

APPLE NUT RING

Judith Grant

2 (8 oz.) refrigerated buttermilk
   biscuits
¾ c. sugar
1 T. cinnamon
½ stick butter or margarine,
   melted

2 med. Granny Smith apples,
   peeled & cored, thin sliced
⅓ c. chopped nuts
¼ c. raisins or craisins
   (cranberries dried)

Separate biscuits into 20 pieces. Combine sugar and cinnamon. Dip biscuits into melted butter. Roll in sugar mixture. Arrange biscuits around deep dish (9-inch baking) using 15; overlap remaining 5 biscuits in center. Place sliced apples between each biscuit and all around outer edge of deep dish. Mix nuts and raisins with remaining sugar mixture and pour over all. Bake at 400° for 25 to 30 minutes. Makes 20 rolls.

APPLE STRUDEL - HUNGARIAN-STYLE

Lorraine Mondulick

1 box strudel or phyllo dough
1 c. bread crumbs
½ c. sugar
3 apples, grated

2 T. cinnamon
½ c. raisins
1 c. walnuts chopped
1 egg, lightly beaten

Place cloth on a table top. Put six layers of pastry dough on cloth. Brush dough lightly with melted butter. Sprinkle with bread crumbs, sugar, apples, cinnamon, raisins and walnuts. Cover with six more layer of dough. Using the cloth under the dough, roll it up loosely. Brush with beaten egg and place on a greased baking tray. Bake at 375° oven for 30 to 40 minutes. Serves 6.

KELLY'S BRAN MUFFINS

Kelly Hunt

2½ c. all-purpose flour
2 T. baking powder
1 T. cinnamon
1 tsp. nutmeg
½ tsp. salt
3 eggs or ¾ egg substitute
½ c. vegetable oil
2 tsp. vanilla

3 well-mashed ripe bananas
1 c. fresh, frozen or strained
  canned blueberries
4 c. Kellogg's All-Bran cereal
2 c. skim milk
⅔ c. dark brown sugar
⅔ c. unsweetened applesauce

Mix cereal, skim milk, brown sugar, cinnamon, nutmeg, eggs, oil, vanilla and bananas. Let set for a minimum of one hour, then add flour, baking powder and salt. Mix well; fold in blueberries prior to cooking. Coat muffin tin with cooking spray and fill approximately ⅔ full. Bake at 350° for 20 to 25 minutes. Makes 24 muffins. Can be frozen and heated in microwave for 45 seconds. Mix can be kept overnight in refrigerator. Other fruits, raisins or shredded carrots can be used.

OATMEAL BRAN MUFFINS

Dolores Whittum

1 c. oatmeal
1 c. All-Bran
1¼ c. buttermilk OR sour milk
1 lg. egg, beaten
¾ c. brown sugar
½ c. vegetable oil

1¼ c. flour
¼ tsp. salt
1-1¼ tsp. baking powder
½ tsp. baking soda
½-¾ c. cut-up dates

Preheat oven to 400°. Spray pans. Put oatmeal, bran and milk in large mixing bowl. Add egg, brown sugar, oil and beat well. Add flour, salt, baking powder, baking soda and dates. Mix slightly. Sprinkle with sugar and cinnamon.

RAISIN BRAN MUFFINS

Fran Moorehead

2½ c. flour
1½ c. sugar
2½ tsp. baking soda
¾ tsp. salt

3¾ c. raisin bran cereal
2 c. buttermilk
½ c. vegetable oil
2 eggs, beaten

Blend flour, sugar, baking soda and salt. Add cereal, mix. Add buttermilk, oil and beaten eggs. Mix until well blended. Bake at 400° for 15 to 20 minutes. Batter may be stored in a plastic container up to 6 weeks.

34808-00

OVERNITE BUTTERSCOTCH BREAKFAST ROLLS

Lorraine Mondulick

1 pkg. frozen rolls
½ (3.4-oz.) pkg. butterscotch
  pudding (not instant)
½ stick margarine

½ tsp. cinnamon
½ c. brown sugar
½ c. chopped nuts

Arrange half package of rolls in greased bundt pan. Sprinkle half of pudding on top of rolls. Arrange rest of rolls, sprinkle remaining pudding. Heat butter, brown sugar and cinnamon until bubbly. Add nuts, pour over rolls. Cover with foil leave on counter overnight. Remove foil, bake at 350° for 30 minutes. Let stand 5 minutes, before inverting on plate. Serve.

CINNAMON BUNS

Diane Neal

8 Rich's frozen rolls
1 pkg. vanilla pudding
½ c. brown sugar

½ c. melted butter
Raisins and/or nuts
Cinnamon

Butter tube pan. Sprinkle raisins and/or nuts in pan. Roll frozen rolls in cinnamon and arrange them in a single, solid ring in bottom of pan. Sprinkle dry pudding mix over rolls (not instant pudding). Sprinkle brown sugar, then pour melted butter over rolls. Cover with towel and let set overnight or at least 8 hours. Bake at 350° for 25 to 30 minutes.

CRESCENT ROLL BREAKFAST CHEESECAKE

Shirley Grube

2 pkgs. crescent rolls
2 (8-oz.) pkgs. cream cheese
¾ c. sugar

2 egg yolks
1 tsp. vanilla
1 tsp. lemon juice

Pat rolls (1 package) into 9 x 13-inch pan. Mix cream cheese, sugar, egg yolks, vanilla and lemon juice. Spread mixture over rolls and pat other package of rolls together over cheese mixture. Bake at 350° oven about 25 minutes or until brown. Dust with powdered sugar.

BLUEBERRY YOGURT WAFFLES

Kelly Hunt

4 T. melted butter (¹/₂ stick)
1³/₄ c. all-purpose flour
1¹/₂ tsp. baking powder
¹/₄ tsp. baking soda
¹/₈ tsp. cinnamon
¹/₃ c. sugar
1 c. plain yogurt (do not use nonfat)

1 c. skim milk
2 lg. eggs or ¹/₂ c. egg substitute such as EggBeaters
1 tsp. pure vanilla extract
1 c. blueberries (fresh, frozen or canned if well rinsed & drained)
Maple syrup for topping

Whisk together all ingredients except blueberries and melted butter. Blend until smooth. Gently fold in blueberries and butter. Spray waffle maker with cooking spray or brush with oil. Pour approximately ¹/₂ cup batter for each waffle. Allow 3 to 4 minutes for cooking. Waffles can be kept in a 200° oven directly on racks to be kept warm.

MAPLE FRENCH TOAST BAKE

Aline Grojean

6-9 (4 x 3 x 1-inch) slices French bread*
3-oz. pkg. cream cheese, softened**
¹/₂ tsp. cinnamon
¹/₄ c. salted margarine, melted

1 c. milk
¹/₃ c. maple syrup
3 eggs
1 T. sugar
1¹/₂ tsp. cinnamon
1 tsp. vanilla

Heat oven to 400°. Spread cream cheese on both sides of French bread slices and place in greased 13 x 9-inch baking pan. Sprinkle ¹/₂ teaspoon cinnamon evenly over bread slices. In medium bowl whisk together all remaining ingredients until well mixed. Pour over bread. Bake for 18 to 20 minutes or until puffy and set. Serve immediately with maple syrup. Yield: 6 servings. *Use as many slices of French bread as needed to cover bottom of 13 x 9-inch pan. ** Three-ounce package Neufchatel cheese (light cream cheese) can be substituted of 3-ounce package cream cheese.

BAKED PANCAKES

Pauline Bridge

¹/₂ stick butter
¹/₂ c. flour
¹/₂ c. milk
Juice of ¹/₂ lemon

Powdered sugar
2 slightly beaten eggs
Pinch salt
Pinch nutmeg

Melt butter in large skillet. Mix don't beat flour, milk, eggs, salt and nutmeg. Pour in skillet. Bake at 425° for 20 to 25 minutes. Remove

(continued)

34808-00

from pan and sprinkle with powdered sugar and juice of ½ lemon. Cut like pie.

"MGO BLUE" BANANA PANCAKES

Steve Levine
Richard Frey

Dry Ingredients:

¾ c. unbleached all-purpose flour
¼ c. buckwheat flour
¼ c. whole-wheat flour
2 T. cornmeal (opt.)

1 T. sugar
1½ tsp. baking powder
½ tsp. baking soda
½ tsp. salt
1½ tsp. cinnamon

Wet Ingredients:

2 eggs
2 T. melted butter
1-1½ c. whole milk

1 c. fresh blueberries
1 THINLY sliced banana

Mix the dry ingredients together in a medium-size bowl. In a separate bowl beat eggs with one cup of milk and melted butter. Add this wet mixture to dry mixture to obtain a basic pancake batter. Add the additional ½ cup milk if mixture is too thick. Stir gently or pancake will toughen. When batter is ready, fold in blueberries. Slice bananas on top of each pancake that is cooking. Makes 8 (5-inch) pancakes.

Recipe Favorites

Recipe Favorites

34808-00

Pies, Pastry & Desserts

Helpful Hints

- Egg whites need to be at room temperature for greater volume when whipped. Remember this when making meringue.

- When preparing several batches of pie dough, roll dough out between sheets of plastic wrap. Stack the discs in a pizza box, and keep the box in the freezer. Next time you're making pie, pull out the required crusts.

- Place your pie plate on a cake stand when placing the pie dough in it and fluting the edges. The cake stand will make it easier to turn the pie plate, and you won't have to stoop over.

- Many kitchen utensils can be used to make decorative pie edges. For a scalloped edge, use a spoon. Crosshatched and herringbone patterns are achieved with a fork. For a sharply pointed effect, use a can opener to cut out points around the rim.

- Dipping strawberries in chocolate? Stick toothpicks into the stem end of the berry. Coat the berries with chocolate, shaking off any excess. Turn the berries upside down and stick the toothpick into a block of styrofoam until the chocolate is set. The finished berries will have chocolate with no flat spots. Another easy solution is to place dipped berries dipped-side up in the holes of an egg carton.

- Keep strawberries fresh for up to ten days by refrigerating them (unwashed) in an airtight container between layers of paper towels.

- When grating citrus peel, bits of peel are often stuck in the holes of the grater. Rather than waste the peel, you can easily brush it off by using a clean toothbrush.

- To core a pear, slice the pear in half lengthwise. Use a melon baller to cut out the central core, using a circular motion. Draw the melon baller to the top of the pear, removing the interior stem as you go.

- When cutting up dried fruit, it sometimes sticks to the blade of the knife. To prevent this problem, coat the blade of your knife with a thin film of vegetable spray before cutting.

- Cutting dessert bars is easier if you score the bars as soon as the pan comes out of the oven. When the bars cool, cut along the scored lines.

- When cutting butter into flour for pastry dough, the process is made easier if you cut the butter into small pieces before adding it to the flour.

KEY LIME PIE

Darlene Jenny

1 (8-inch) graham cracker crust
4 egg yolks, lightly beaten
½ c. sugar
⅓ c. freshly squeezed Key lime
  juice
2¼ tsp. grated Key lime zest
2¼ c. heavy cream

In the top of a double boiler, combine the egg yolks, sugar and lime juice. Cook the mixture over moderate heat for about 10 minutes, until it coats the back of a spoon. Remove from the heat and stir in the grated zest. Chill until the mixture thickens, but don't let it become stiff. Whip 1½ cups of the cream to soft peaks and fold into lime filling. Spoon into the pie crust and chill, covered, 24 hours. **To serve:** Whip the remaining ¾ cup cream and spread on the filling.

QUICK AND EASY KEY LIME PIE

Sherie Becker

1 can sweetened condensed
  milk
8 oz. sour cream
⅓ c. **Nellie & Joe's Key lime**
  juice
Graham cracker crust
Whipped cream

Stir sweetened condensed milk and sour cream. Add Key lime juice. Chill for at least one hour. Top with whipped cream.

STRAWBERRY PIE

Joan Racelis

1½ c. water
2 T. cornstarch
4 pkgs. Equal
1 (3-oz.) pkg. sugar free Jello
  (strawberry)
4 c. fresh strawberries, sliced

In medium saucepan, mix water and cornstarch; cook over medium heat until bubbles form, stirring constantly. Remove from heat. Sprinkle sugar substitute and gelatin over mixture; stir in and let cool. Then fold in strawberries and pour into graham cracker crust. Refrigerate. Can serve with whipped cream.

RHUBARB CUSTARD PIE

Ginny Moss

4 c. fresh rhubarb, cut into
 ½-inch pieces
1 unbaked 9-inch pie shell
1 c. sugar

1 T. all-purpose flour
¼ tsp. ground nutmeg
4 slightly beaten eggs

Place rhubarb is pastry shell. Combine sugar, flour and nutmeg. Add eggs, beat well. Pour egg mixture into pastry shell. To prevent over-browning, cover edge with foil. Bake in 375° oven for 25 minutes. Remove foil; bake 20 minutes more or until pie is set. Cool, cover; store in refrigerator.

LEMON CUSTARD AND STRAWBERRY SUPREME PIE

Kati Parker

Pastry for 1 (9-inch) pie or
 ready-made shell
½ c. sugar (granulated)
4 tsp. cornstarch
½ c. water
1 beaten egg yolk
2 T. butter

3 T. lemon juice
3 c. sliced fresh strawberries
2 (3-oz.) cream cheese, softened
¼ c. sifted powdered sugar
⅓ c. flaked coconut
1 pt. whipping cream
¼ c. flaked coconut, toasted

In a saucepan combine granulated sugar and cornstarch. Add water, egg yolk and butter. Cook and stir until thickened and bubbly; cook 2 minutes more. Remove from heat. Stir in lemon juice. Turn into baked shell, set aside to cool. Top this with sliced strawberries. In a small mixer bowl, beat cream cheese and powdered sugar. Fold in ⅓ cup coconut. In another bowl, beat whipped cream cheese and powdered sugar. Fold in ⅓ cup coconut. In another bowl, beat whipped cream to soft peaks and fold into cream cheese mixture until combined. Spread on top of berries. Sprinkle with ¼ cup toasted coconut. Chill 4 hours or overnight.

JIMMY'S PEACHES AND CREAM PIE

Sonya Smetzer

¾ c. flour
1 tsp. baking powder
½ tsp. salt
1 (3-oz.) box vanilla pudding
 (NOT INSTANT)
3 T. melted butter
1 lg. egg
½ c. milk

1-lb. can drained, sliced
 peaches
8 oz. cream cheese
½ c. sugar
3 T. peach juice
1 T. sugar
½ tsp. cinnamon

(continued)

34808-00

Mix for 2 minutes: flour, 1 teaspoon baking powder, ½ teaspoon salt, vanilla pudding, butter and milk. Spread mixture into a 9-inch greased glass or ceramic pie pan. Over the top spread sliced peaches, in wheel-fashion. (Save the juice.) Mix cream cheese, sugar and peach juice. Beat 2 minutes. Spread over the peaches all the way over to the edge of the pan. Mix sugar and cinnamon, sprinkle over the pie. Bake at 350° for 30 minutes. Chill few hours or overnight.

CORA'S COMPANY PIE

Helen Cueto

½ c. butter or margarine
¾ c. sugar
2 eggs, unbeaten
½ tsp. cinnamon
½ tsp. nutmeg

¼ tsp. salt
1 tsp. vinegar
½ c. chopped nuts
½ c. raisins
9-inch pastry shell

Combine butter, sugar and eggs. Beat well. Add cinnamon, nutmeg, salt, vinegar, nuts and raisins. Put into pie shell and bake at 400° for about 30 minutes.

CRUSTLESS MILKTART

Robert J. Woyciechowski

3 T. melted butter
3 eggs, separated
1 c. sugar
1 c. flour
1 tsp. baking powder

¾ tsp. salt
1 tsp. vanilla
4 c. whole milk
Cinnamon/sugar, mixed

Mix butter, egg yolks and sugar. Sift flour, baking powder and salt, then add. Add vanilla and milk. Beat egg whites and fold in. Pour into deep, greased pie plate and sprinkle with cinnamon/sugar mixture. Bake a total of 40 minutes. Start at 375° for 25 minutes or until set, then reduce to 325°. Serve hot or cold.

CHOCOLATE NUT PIE

Doris Coones

2 eggs, lightly beaten
¼ lb. butter, melted & cooled
1 c. sugar
1 tsp. vanilla

1 c. English walnuts
1 c. chocolate chips
1 unbaked pie shell

Mix eggs, butter, sugar, vanilla, walnuts and chips. Pour into unbaked pie shell. Bake 30 minutes in 375° oven.

ITALIAN EASTER PIE

Linda DeRogatis

3 lbs. ricotta
6 eggs, beaten
1/3-1/2 lb. salami, chopped
  coarsely
1 lb. shredded mozzarella
1/2 lb. prosciutto, chopped
  coarsely
1/4 lb. Swiss cheese, chopped
  coarsely

1/4 c. grated Pecorino Romano
  cheese
2 hard-boiled eggs, sliced
1/4 c. chopped Italian parsley
Black pepper
2 deep dish pie shells with tops

Mix all above ingredients by hand. Preheat oven to 375°. Place 2 uncooked pie shells on cookie sheet, fill shells. Cover with top pie shells. Brush tops generously with a beaten egg and one ice cube. Make slits in crust to vent heat. Brush again 3/4 through cooking. Bake 1 hour or until golden brown. Makes 2 pies. Freezes well.

ZEPPOLE
(Fried Puffs of Dough)

Jo Russo

1 pkg. active dry yeast
1 c. warm water
1 egg

2 T. sugar
2 1/2 c. all-purpose flour
1/2 tsp. salt

Sprinkle yeast in to warm water. Stir to dissolve and let stand for a few minutes before proceeding with rest of mixing. Break egg into yeast, add sugar, then flour sifted into mixture, then salt. Stir well. When smooth, beat with hand, cover and let stand in a warm place until bubbly and double in bulk. Beat again and let rise again until double. Rising will take about 3 hours, but can be left longer. When ready heat oil in deep fryer to 400°. Oil depth should be at least 3 inches. Drop dough by teaspoonful into hot oil. When golden on one side turn over. Drain on paper and sprinkle with confectioners' sugar. Makes about 35.

FLAN

Lorraine Mondulick

2 c. sugar
1/2 c. water
8 lg. eggs
2 tsp. vanilla

Pinch of salt
1 (10-inch) round cake pan
1 (12-inch) round cake pan

In a heavy saucepan over moderate heat stir together 1 cup sugar and 1/2 cup water until dissolved. Cook until golden brown without stirring. Pour syrup into a 10-inch cake pan; tilt to coat bottom and sides. Let cool 30 minutes. Heat milk until lukewarm. In large bowl beat together

(continued)

34808-00

eggs, remaining sugar, vanilla and salt until blended. Slowly add 1 cup lukewarm milk. Add remaining milk and beat to blend. Place mixture in the 10-inch round pan slowly. Place the 10-inch pan inside the 12-inch round pan. Pour enough water in the 12-inch pan to come up as high as the custard mixture in the 10-inch pan. Bake in a preheated 350° oven until a knife inserted comes out clean. Allow to cool overnight. Invert to a large flat bowl with sides to catch the syrup. Serve with whipped cream.

FLAN

Andrea Junghans

4 (14-oz.) cans sweetened
  condensed milk (rinse can)
4 (14-oz.) cans milk (rinse can)
8 eggs

1 oz. rum
2 T. vanilla extract (good
  quality)
2 c. sugar

In metal cake pan (13 x 9 inches) caramelize 2 cups sugar over burner. Set aside. Mix milks, eggs, rum and vanilla. Pour into metal pan. Bake 1 hour at 350° in water bath until knife comes out clean. Custard will set in refrigerator. Turn over onto platter. Decorate with maraschino cherries

EGGNOG PUDDING WITH RASPBERRY SAUCE

Leslie McQueen

3 T. plain gelatin (3 env.)
½ c. cold water
1 qt. dairy eggnog

2 T. rum
2 c. whipping cream, whipped

Soften gelatin in cold water. Heat 1 cup of eggnog to boiling. Add gelatin and stir until dissolved. Add remaining eggnog and rum. Chill until partially thickened. Fold in whipping cream. Pour into individual molds or ring-mold. Refrigerate overnight.

Raspberry Sauce:

1 lb. frozen raspberries, thawed
½ c. sugar

1 T. rum
2 T. cornstarch

Cook raspberries to boiling. Force through a fine sieve. Return to pan. Cook to boiling again. Mix sugar and cornstarch and stir into raspberries, stirring constantly until thickened and clear. Add rum.

Note: Alcohol in rum cooks down. Chill well. Drizzle over unmolded Eggnog Pudding. Garnish with mint leaves. Serve rest of sauce on side.

BREAD PUDDING

Jo Russo

20 slices white bread (store brand is best)
½ gal. milk
1 c. sugar
1 tsp. salt
7 lg. eggs

1 stick butter, cut into sm. pieces
¼ c. pancake syrup
Whipped cream for topping (opt.)

Grease inside of a (2 x 9 x 13-inch) Pyrex pan. Tear bread into small pieces. Place in pan. Blend together, milk, sugar, salt and eggs in a bowl. Using a ladle, slowly pour mixture over bread, a little at a time, pressing down gently to soak bread, if poured too much at once, it will overflow. Dot top with butter pieces and sprinkle pancake syrup. Place in a cold oven, then turn oven to 350° and bake 1½ hours. Place a cookie sheet or foil under pan to catch any drippings. When first removing from oven, the pudding may be a little loose, but will thicken as it cools.

FLUFFY RICE DESSERT

Dorothy Roehr

1 (3-oz.) pkg. sugar-free cherry gelatin
1 c. boiling water
1 (20-oz.) can unsweetened crushed pineapple

1½ c. hot cooked rice
1 c. light whipped topping

In a bowl, dissolve gelatin in boiling water. Drain pineapple, reserving juice, set pineapple aside. Add juice to gelatin, stir in rice. Chill until mixture begins to thicken. Fold in whipped topping and pineapple. Chill for one hour.

LEMON SQUARES

Shirley Cote

Crust:

1½ c. flour
⅓ c. brown sugar

¾ c. margarine
½ c. nuts

Filling:

1 (8 oz.) cream cheese
1 c. confectioners' sugar

1 c. whipped topping from a 9-oz. ctn.

Topping:

3 c. cold milk

2 pkgs. instant lemon pudding

Combine all crust ingredients. (flour, sugar, margarine and nuts); press in bottom of 13 x 9-inch pan. Bake at 375° for 15 minutes. Cool. Blend all

(continued)

34808-00

ingredients for filling (cream cheese, confectioners' sugar and whipped topping); spread on cooled crust. Mix topping (milk and pudding); let set up. Spread in pan. Cover with remaining whipped topping. Garnish with chopped nuts. Refrigerate.

PEACH OR BLUEBERRY COBBLER

Michelle James

2 c. any berries or peaches
  (sweeten with sugar)
1 stick butter
¾ c. flour

¾ c. sugar
¾ c. milk
Pinch of salt
1 tsp. baking powder

Melt butter in baking dish. Make batter of flour, sugar, milk, salt and baking powder. Put batter in baking dish. Place berries on top of batter. Batter will rise to top. Bake at 350° for 30 minutes.

PINK FLUFF

Linda Kammerer

1 box raspberry Jello
1 c. hot water
1 sm. can crushed pineapple,
  drained

1 pkg. cream cheese
½ pt. whipping cream
1 c. chopped nuts

Dissolve Jello in hot water and place in refrigerator. When Jello begins to congeal, add well-drained pineapple and cream cheese which has been mashed with fork. Whip cream until stiff and stir in nuts. Fold all together and place in a salad mold or individual molds. Serves 8 and doubles easily.

PUMPKIN CHIFFON DESSERT

Pauline Bridge

1¾ c. graham cracker crumbs
¼ c. sugar
½ c. butter, melted
1 (8-oz.) pkg. cream cheese,
  softened
Dash cinnamon
½ c. chopped pecans
2 eggs, beaten

¾ c. sugar
2 (3¾-oz.) pkgs. vanilla instant
  pudding
¾ c. milk
2 c. cooked mashed pumpkin
1 (8-oz.) ctn. frozen whipped
  topping, thawed & divided

Combine crumbs, batter and sugar; press into 13 x 9 x 2-inch pan. Combine cream cheese, eggs and ¾ cup sugar. Beat until fluffy. Spread over crust. Bake 20 minutes at 350°. Cool. Combine pudding mix and milk, beat 2 minutes on medium speed. Add pumpkin and cinnamon; mix well. Stir in 1 cup whipped topping. Spread pudding mixture over

(continued)

cream cheese layer. Chill and spread remaining topping over top. Sprinkle top with pecans. Refrigerate. Serves 15.

FRUIT AND ANGEL TRIFLE

Angela Smith

1 lg. angel food cake, cut into bite-size pieces
15-oz. can crushed pineapple, undrained
6-oz. jar maraschino cherries, chopped & drained
12-oz. ctn. Cool Whip
3½-oz. can flaked coconut

Layer ½ of cake into a 13 x 9-inch glass trifle bowl. Top with ½ pineapple, cherries and Cool Whip. Repeat layers. Toast coconut and sprinkle over top layer of Cool Whip. Cover, refrigerate overnight. Serves 12.

RASPBERRY CHEESECAKE TRIFLE

Charlotte Appledorn

1 (9-oz.) pkg. white cake mix
1 (8-oz.) pkg. cream cheese, softened
¼ c. confectioners' sugar
1½ c. whipping cream, whipped
3 c. fresh raspberries
2 (1-oz.) sq. semi-sweet chocolate, coarsely grated

Prepare and bake cake mix according to directions. Cool; cut into 1-inch cubes. In small mixing bowl, beat cream cheese and sugar until smooth. Fold in whipped cream. In a trifle bowl, layer half of the cake cubes, 1 cup of raspberries, half the cream cheese mix and half the chocolate. Repeat layers. Top with the remaining raspberries. Refrigerate for 4 hours or overnight.

WHIP CREAM CHARLOTTE

Maria Elena Bruno

16 oz. cream cheese
¾ c. sugar
1½ pt. whipping cream
1 tsp. vanilla
2 pkgs. lady fingers
1 can pie filling or fresh fruit

Beat cream cheese with sugar and vanilla until light and creamy. In separate bowl whip cream. Fold together. Line a spring pan bottom and sides with lady fingers. Pour in cream mixture and refrigerate overnight. Garnish with fresh fruit and glaze or can pie filling.

34808-00

VANILLA FRUIT

Nan Kostura

1 can pineapple chunks
1 can fruit cocktail
1 can mandarin oranges
1 lg. pkg. instant vanilla pie
  filling

1 jar maraschino cherries,
  chopped
3 bananas, chopped

Mix vanilla pie and pudding filling with pineapple chunks and juice. Drain fruit cocktail, mandarin oranges and cherries. Refrigerate. Add bananas before serving or any other fresh fruit, as sliced grapes, sliced strawberries or peaches.

RASPBERRY MOUSSE

June Zuranski

1 env. (1 T.) gelatin
1/3 c. orange juice
2 pkgs. frozen raspberries
2 T. fruit liquor

2 egg whites
1 1/2 c. heavy cream, whipped
1/4 c. sugar

Soften gelatin in the orange juice. Drain raspberries. Measure juice and add enough water to make 1 cup liquid. Cook juice and sugar over low heat until syrupy. Add berries and cook 10 minutes. Add gelatin and mix until dissolved. Force through a strainer. Cool. Add liquor. Beat egg whites. Fold into berry purée. Beat cream and fold into berry mixture. Pour into a 1 1/2-quart mold and chill until firm. Serves 6 to 8.

HEALTHY MOUSSE

Suzanne Kinder

1 pkg. instant pudding mix
1 1/3 c. skim milk
8 oz. yogurt

1 loaf angel food cake
1-2 c. fruit

You may use any combination of pudding and yogurt. Tear cake into bite-sized pieces. Put in serving bowl. Sprinkle pudding over milk in medium mixing bowl and beat 30 seconds. Add yogurt and beat another 30 seconds. Put fruit on top of cake and pour pudding mix over.

KATHY'S CARAMEL PECAN ICE CREAM DELIGHT

Kathy Tudyk

1 c. flour
1 stick butter, melted

1 jar Kraft caramel
1/2 gal. vanilla ice cream

1/4 c. chopped pecans
1/4 c. brown sugar

Cool Whip
Tia Maria

(continued)

Mix flour, butter, pecans, brown sugar and spread onto cookie sheet. Bake 15 to 20 minutes or until brown at 350°. Cool and crumble. Spread ½ of mixture in 9 x 13-inch pan. Pour 1 jar caramel sauce onto mixture. Spread softened ice cream over sauce. Sprinkle remaining mixture on top. Freeze. Onto each serving pour 1 teaspoon Tia Maria and top with Cool Whip.

MAMA'S MINTED PEARS
(Company Dish)

Selda Berns

Canned Bartlett pear halves (2
  halves per serving)
Juice from ½ lemon
½ c. sugar
Fresh drops peppermint oil or
  green creme de menthe

Green food coloring
Canned grated coconut
Jar of cherries

Day before serving, pour pear juice into stewing pot, add lemon juice, sugar and few drops peppermint oil and enough food coloring to give lovely green color. (Be cautious with oil, little goes long way!) Can substitute green creme de menthe for sugar and peppermint oil. Then use less coloring. Boil uncovered 10 minutes and cool. Put pears in flat dish, pour juice over them. Refrigerate. Turn often so color will be even. **To serve:** Fill centers with coconut; top with cherry.

CREAM PUFF SHELLS

Linda Kammerer

1 c. water
½ butter
⅛ tsp. salt
1 c. sifted flour

4 eggs
Whipped cream or custard
  pudding

Place water, butter and salt in heavy saucepan and heat. When boiling, add flour all at once. Stir vigorously with a wooden spoon. Beat until mixture forms a smooth ball which leaves sides of pan clean, stirring constantly. Remove from stove. Beat in one egg at a time. Continue beating until mixture is thick and smooth and breaks off when spoon is raised. Shape at once or wrap dough in waxed paper and store in refrigerator before using. With tablespoon shape on greased baking sheet, putting shape 2 inches apart to allow for spreading. **For Cream Puff Shells:** Make large rounds, for eclairs, make 1 x 4½-inch strips. Bake large puffs in a 450° for 15 minutes, then reduce heat to 350° and bake 20 to 25 minutes longer. Bake miniature shells about ½ the time. Cut slit in side and fill with whipped cream or your favorite custard or pudding. Sprinkle tops with powdered sugar.

34808-00

NEVER FAIL PIE CRUST

Katie Parker

4 c. flour
2 T. sugar
2 T. salt
1³/₄ c. vegetable shortening

½ c. cold water
1 T. vinegar
1 egg

Using pastry cutter, blend 1³/₄ cups shortening, flour, sugar and salt. Add water, vinegar and egg. Chill 1 hour; roll out on lightly floured board.

Recipe Favorites

Recipe Favorites

34808-00

Cakes, Cookies & Candy

Helpful Hints

- Push animal shaped cookie cutters lightly into icing on cakes or cupcakes. Fill depressed outlines with chocolate icing or decorating confections.

- Fill flat bottomed ice cream cones half full with cake batter and bake. Top with icing and decorating confections.

- Marshmallows can be used for candle holders on cakes.

- To keep the cake plate clean while frosting, slide 6-inch strips of waxed paper under each side of the cake. Once the cake is frosted and the frosting is set, pull the strips away leaving a clean plate.

- When decorating a cake with chocolate, you can make a quick decorating tube. Put chocolate in a heat-safe zipper-lock plastic bag. Immerse in simmering water until the chocolate is melted. Snip off the tip of one corner, and you can squeeze the chocolate out of the bag.

- Professionally decorated cakes have a silky, molten look. To get that appearance, frost your cake as usual, then use a hair dryer to blow-dry the surface. The slight melting of the frosting will give it that lustrous appearance.

- To ensure that you have equal amounts of batter in each pan when making a layered cake, use a kitchen scale to measure the weight.

- To make cookie crumbs for your recipes, put cookies into a plastic bag and run a rolling pin back and forth until they are the right size.

- To decorate cookies with chocolate, place cookies on a rack over waxed paper. Dip the tines of a fork with chocolate, and wave the fork gently back and forth making wavy lines.

- A gadget that works well for decorating sugar cookies is an empty plastic thread spool. Simply press the spool into the dough, imprinting a pretty flower design.

- Some holiday cookies require an indent on top to fill with jam or chocolate. Use the rounded end of a honey dipper to make the indent.

- When a recipe calls for packed brown sugar, fill the correct size measuring cup with the sugar, and then use the next smaller size cup to pack the brown sugar into its cup.

BLACK RUSSIAN CAKE

Helen Cueto

1 pkg. dark chocolate cake mix
1 c. vegetable oil
1 (3-oz.) pkg. instant chocolate
  pudding

4 eggs
¾ c. strong coffee
½ c. creme de cacao
¼ c. Kahlua

For Topping:

1 c. powdered sugar, sifted
2 T. strong coffee

2 T. Kahlua
2 T. creme de cacao

Preheat oven to 350°. Combine cake mix, vegetable oil, pudding, eggs, coffee, creme de cacao, Kahlua in a large bowl. Beat 4 minutes until quite smooth. Pour into a greased 10-inch tube pan until ¾ full. Bake 45 to 50 minutes. Remove from pan and invert onto serving plate. Punch holes throughout the cake with a skewer on ice pick. Combine all the topping ingredients in a bowl. Mix well and spoon over the cake and into holes.

BLACK MAGIC CAKE

Lorraine McCullough

1¾ c. unsifted flour
2 c. sugar
¾ c. unsweetened cocoa
1 tsp. salt
1 tsp. baking soda
1 tsp. baking powder

2 eggs
1 c. strong black coffee
1 c. buttermilk
½ c. vegetable oil
1 tsp. vanilla

Grease and flour pans. Thoroughly combine flour, salt, sugar, cocoa, baking powder and soda. Add eggs, coffee, buttermilk, vegetable oil and vanilla all at once. Beat 2 minutes with electric mixer on medium speed. Batter should be thin. Bake at 350° for 30 to 35 minutes for a 9-inch layer, 35 to 40 minutes for a 13 x 9-inch pan. Cool 10 minutes in the pan. Let cool completely to frost.

TRIPLE CHOCOLATE CAKE

Fran Morehead

1 pkg. chocolate cake mix
1 pkg. chocolate instant
  pudding mix

1¾ c. milk
2 eggs
1 (12-oz.) pkg. chocolate chips

Combine all ingredients in large mixing bowl and stir with big spoon for 2 minutes. Pour mixture into greased bundt pan. Bake at 350° for 50

(continued)

to 55 minutes. Cool cake 15 minutes before removing from pan. If desired, sprinkle with powdered sugar.

CHOCOLATE TEXAS SHEET CAKE

Pauline Bridge

1 c. water or coffee	2 tsp. soda
½ lb. margarine	½ tsp. salt
2 heaping tsp. cocoa	2 eggs
2 c. sifted flour	½ c. buttermilk
2 c. sugar	1 tsp. vanilla
1½ tsp. cinnamon	

Bring to boil water and margarine. Pour over flour, sugar, cinnamon, soda and salt. Add eggs, buttermilk and vanilla. Beat 2 minutes. Pour into greased and floured large sheet pan (10 x 15 x 1 inch). Bake 25 minutes at 350°.

BACARDI RUM CAKE

Ethel Rudy

1 c. chopped pecans or walnuts	4 eggs
1 (18½-oz.) pkg. yellow cake mix	½ c. cold water
	½ c. salad oil
1 (3¾-oz.) pkg. vanilla instant pudding	½ c. Bacardi dark rum (80 proof)

Glaze:

¼ lb. butter	½ c. Bacardi dark rum (80 proof)
¼ c. water	
1 c. granulated sugar	

Preheat oven to 325°. Grease and flour 10-inch tube or 12-cup bundt pan. Sprinkle nuts over bottom of pan. Mix together cake mix, pudding, eggs, water, salad oil and rum. Pour butter over nuts. Bake 1 hour. Cool. Invert on serving plate. Prick top. Drizzle and smooth glaze evenly over top and sides. Allow cake to absorb glaze. Repeat until glaze is used up. **Glaze:** Melt butter in saucepan. Stir in water and sugar. Boil 5 minutes, stirring constantly. Remove from heat. Stir in rum.

BOURBON CAKE

Michelle James

2 c. butter	2 or 2½ tsp. vanilla
3 c. sugar	2½ jiggers (7 T.) bourbon whiskey
8 eggs, separated	
3 c. flour (use all-purpose flour & sift before measuring)	½ c. or more finely ground pecans

(continued)

34808-00

Cream butter, then gradually add sugar, beating until fluffy. Add egg yolks one at at time, beating well after each egg. Then continue to beat until light and fluffy, do not under beat! Add flour along with flavoring and bourbon. Fold in stiffly beaten egg whites and nuts. Grease large tube pan, line bottom with wax paper. Spread bottom of pan with layer of ground nuts, then add batter and bake 1½ hours at 320°.

MEXICAN WEDDING CAKE

Kelly Hunt

2 c. sugar
2 eggs, well beaten or ½ c. egg
  substitute
1 (20-oz.) can crushed pineapple
  with juice

2 c. flour
2 tsp. baking soda
1 c. chopped nuts

Frosting:

4 oz. butter
1 (8-oz.) pkg. cream cheese

1 tsp. vanilla
1½ c. powdered sugar

Preheat oven to 350°. Mix all cake ingredients in a large mixing bowl. Pour into ungreased 9 x 13-inch pan. Bake for 30 to 35 minutes. While cake is cooling, mix together frosting ingredients with electric mixer until consistency is smooth and creamy. Spread evenly over cake when completely cooled. Cover and store in refrigerator.

ITALIAN CREAM CAKE

Charlotte Appledorn

1 stick butter
½ c. shortening
5 eggs, separated
2 c. flour
1 tsp. baking soda

1 c. buttermilk
1 tsp. vanilla
1 can flaked coconut
½ c. pecans, chopped

Frosting:

1½ pkgs. creamed cheese
½ stick butter
1 lb. powdered sugar

1 tsp. vanilla
½ c. chopped pecans

Preheat oven to 350°. Grease bottom of 3 pans. Cream together butter, sugar, egg yolks and shortening. Beat egg whites until stiff. Add flour and soda gradually to creamed mixture alternating with buttermilk. Add coconut and pecans. Fold in egg whites. Pour into 3 round layer pans and bake for 25 minutes. **Frosting:** Mix together and frost cake between layers, sides and top.

ITALIAN LOVE CAKE

Marie Elena Bruno

1 box chocolate cake mix

Filling:

¾ c. sugar
3 eggs

1 tsp. vanilla
2 lbs. ricotta cheese

Icing:

1 box chocolate instant pudding
¼ c. powdered sugar

1 c. milk
8 oz. Cool Whip

For Cake: Follow directions on box, except use 1 cup water and ¼ cup club soda. Pour into 9 x 13-inch greased pan. Mix filling and pour over cake batter but leave 1-inch from all sides. Bake at 350° for 60 minutes. Cool completely. **Icing:** Beat together for 1 minute the following 1 box chocolate pudding, ¼ cup powdered sugar and 1 cup milk. Fold in Cool Whip. Leave cake in pan and top with icing. Refrigerate overnight.

AMAZIN' RAISIN CAKE

Helen Cueto

3 c. unsifted flour
2 c. sugar
2 tsp. baking soda
1½ tsp. cinnamon
½ tsp. nutmeg
½ tsp. salt
¼ tsp. cloves
1 c. mayonnaise

⅓ c. milk
2 eggs
3 c. chopped apples
1 c. raisins
1 c. chopped walnuts
1 c. heavy whipping cream,
  whipped

Grease and flour two (9-inch) layer cake pans. In large bowl combine flour, sugar, baking soda, cinnamon, nutmeg, salt and cloves. Add mayonnaise, milk and eggs. Beat at low speed 2 minutes, scraping bowl frequently. (Batter will be thick.) With spoon, stir in apples, raisins and nuts. Spoon into pans. Bake at 350° oven for 40 to 45 minutes or until cake tester inserted in center comes out clean. Cool in pans 10 minutes. Remove; cool on racks. Fill and frost with whipped cream. Serves 12.

34808-00

NORSK JULEKAKA
(Norwegian Christmas Cake)

June Jorgensen

3 eggs
1½ c. sugar
1½ c. milk
5 T. melted butter (margarine o.k.)
1 c. raisins (dark)

½ c. citron or white raisins
4 c. flour
2 T. baking powder
½ tsp. salt
2 tsp. ground cardamon

Beat eggs well with sugar, add milk, melted butter, raisins, citron or white raisins. Sift flour with baking powder, salt and cardamon. Grease two loaf pans well and bake in moderate oven (375°) for 50 minutes. Makes two large loaves or three small, only bake for 45 minutes if using smaller pans.

PINEAPPLE CAKE

Robert J. Woyciechowski

2 c. sugar
2 lg. eggs
1 tsp. vanilla
1 (20-oz.) can crushed pineapple (use all liquid)

2 c. flour
2 tsp. baking soda
½ c. chopped nuts

Frosting:

1 (8 oz.) cream cheese
1 stick butter
1 tsp. vanilla

1¾ c. powdered sugar
½ c. chopped nuts

Mix sugar, eggs, vanilla and pineapple. In separate bowl mix flour and baking soda, then blend in. Add nuts. Pour batter into 9 x 13-inch greased and floured pan. Bake at 350° for 35 to 45 minutes. Let cake cool. Mix frosting ingredients and spread over cake.

MANDARIN ORANGE CAKE

Cheryl E. Martin
Debra Weber

1 (11-oz.) can mandarin oranges, undrained
4 eggs

½ c. oil
1 yellow cake mix

Frosting:

1 box instant vanilla pudding mix
1 (11-oz.) can crushed pineapple, undrained

1 (9-oz.) ctn. Cool Whip

(continued)

Mix oranges, eggs and ½ cup oil. Beat in cake mix. Divide into 3 to 4 cake pans. Bake at 350° for 15 to 20 minutes. Cool cakes. **Frosting:** Mix pudding, pineapple and Cool Whip. Frost each layer. Assemble layers. Refrigerate.

LEMON SNOWBALL CAKE

Kati Parker

2 env. unflavored gelatin
4 T. cold water
1 c. boiling water
1 c. granulated sugar
Dash salt
1 (12-oz.) can frozen orange
  juice concentrate, thawed
2 T. lemon juice
Grated peel of 1 lemon

1 pt. whipping cream (2 c.)
1 (about 10-oz.) angel food cake,
  cut in 1-inch cubes
½ pt. whipping cream (1 c.)
4 T. powdered sugar
1 (4-oz.) pkg. shredded coconut
Green garden leaves such as
  mint
Strawberries

Line a 12-cup bowl with 2 pieces of wax paper, one on top of the other. Let each piece extend over opposite edges of bowl so all edges are covered; paper will be wrinkled. Set bowl aside. In large bowl, sprinkle gelatin over cold water. Let stand 5 minutes to soften. Add boiling water; stir until gelatin is dissolved. Stir in granulated sugar, salt, orange juice concentrate, lemon juice and peel. Refrigerate 45 minutes to 1 hour, stirring occasionally, until partially set and mixture mounds when dropped from a spoon. In a large bowl, whip 1 pint cream until it forms soft peaks. Fold gelatin mixture into whipped cream. Spoon a small amount of lemon mixture into prepared bowl. Scatter several pieces of cake over lemon mixture. Continue alternating cake and lemon mixture until all is used. Cover with plastic wrap and foil. Refrigerate 1 or 2 days before serving. May also be frozen. Thaw in refrigerator overnight. Before serving, invert bowl on serving platter. Carefully remove bowl and wax paper. In a small bowl, whip ½ pint cream and powdered sugar until stiff. Frost top and sides of molded cake with whipped cream. Press coconut into cream. Surround cake with leaves and strawberries. May be refrigerated several hours. Makes 16 servings.

COCONUT CAKE

Rhonda Maule

1 white cake mix
1 (15 oz.) Coca Casa coconut
  (cream of coconut)

1 (16 oz.) Cool Whip
1 sm. pkg. flaked coconut

Mix and bake cake according to package directions. As soon a cake come out of oven; poke holes all over top of cake. Pour on one can of Coco Casa coconut evenly. Refrigerate until cold. Then cover with Cool Whip and coconut. Keep refrigerated.

34808-00

SOUR CREAM POUND CAKE

Angela Smith

2 sticks butter, softened
3 c. sugar
6 eggs
3 c. cake flour

¼ tsp. baking powder
1 tsp. vanilla extract
1 c. sour cream

Preheat oven to 300°. Grease and flour (9-inch) tube or bundt pan. Cream butter and sugar together until light and fluffy. Add eggs, two at a time, beating thoroughly after each addition. Sift cake and baking powder together; add to butter mixture alternately with sour cream, beginning and ending with flour. Blend in vanilla. Bake 1¼ to 1½ hours until the cake shrinks slightly from sides. Cool in pan 10 minutes, then invert on a wire rack turn upright and allow to cool completely.

CHOCOLATE CHIP POUND CAKE

Kathy Price

1 box yellow cake mix
1 (4-serving) box instant
   chocolate pudding
4 eggs

½ c. Crisco oil
1 c. milk
1 (6-oz.) pkg. chocolate chips

Preheat oven to 350°. Grease bundt cake pan (Pam spray). Mix by hand 1 box cake mix, pudding, eggs, oil and milk. Add chocolate chips. Pour into greased cake pan. Bake 45 minutes (use cake tester). Cool. Turn over on plate. Sprinkle with powdered sugar.

CHEESE CAKE

Jan Winn

5 eggs
1½ c. sugar
1¼ lbs. ricotta cheese
2 lg., 1 sm. cream cheese
1 lb. sour cream

3 T. flour
3 T. cornstarch
1 tsp. vanilla
3 T. lemon juice

Preheat oven to 350°. Cream eggs and sugar, then add cream cheese, ricotta, sour cream, cornstarch, flour, vanilla and lemon juice. Pour into greased and floured springform pan. Bake 1 hour or until lightly browned. Turn off oven and let stand with door open. Do not move until cake settles. Remove from oven and refrigerate.

WHITE CHOCOLATE CHEESECAKE

Suzi Massey

2 (8-oz.) pkgs. Philadelphia
  cream cheese, softened
1/2 c. sugar
1/2 tsp. vanilla
2 eggs

4 sq. white baking chocolate,
  chopped, divided or 2/3 c. white
  chocolate chips, divided
1 (9-inch) ready-to-use
  chocolate flavor crumb crust

Mix cream cheese, sugar and vanilla with electric mixer until well blended. Add eggs; mix until blended. Stir in 1/3 cup of the white chocolate. Pour into crust. Sprinkle with remaining white chocolate. Bake at 350° for 35 minutes or until center is almost set. Cool. Refrigerate 3 hours or overnight. Makes 8 servings.

CHOCOLATE RASPBERRY CHEESECAKE

Barbara Limon

1 chocolate-flavored pie crust
  (Keebler)
12 oz. cream cheese, softened
1/2 c. sugar
1/2 tsp. vanilla

2 eggs
1/2 c. frozen raspberries,
  thawed & drained
Glaze (see below)

Preheat oven to 325°. Beat cream cheese until fluffy. Gradually add sugar and vanilla. Add eggs, one at a time, beating after each until well blended. Fold in raspberries. Place crust on baking sheet. Fill with raspberry mixture. Bake for 35 minutes. Cool slightly. **Glaze:** Combine 1 teaspoon butter, 1 ounce unsweetened Hershey's chocolate, 1/4 cup powdered sugar, 1 teaspoon dark corn syrup, 2 teaspoons boiling water over low heat until chocolate is melted. Remove from heat. Stir in 1/2 teaspoon vanilla. Pour over slightly cooled cheesecake and chill 3 hours.

CARROT CAKE

Barbara Ryan

4 eggs
2 c. sugar
3 (4 1/2-oz.) sm. jars strained
  baby carrots
1 (20-oz.) can drained crushed
  pineapple
1 c. chopped nuts

1 c. raisins
1 1/2 c. Wesson oil
2 c. flour
1 tsp. salt
2 tsp. baking soda
2 tsp. cinnamon
2 tsp. vanilla

Mix eggs, sugar, carrots, pineapple, nuts, raisins, oil, flour, salt, baking soda, cinnamon and vanilla well; pour into a greased and floured 13 x 9-inch pan. Bake at 350° for 1 hour.

108

34808-00

CARROT CAKE

Maria Elene Bruno

2 c. flour
2 tsp. baking powder
1½ tsp. baking soda
1½ tsp. salt
2 tsp. cinnamon
2 c. sugar

1½ c. vegetable oil
3 eggs
5 oz. shredded carrots
8 oz. crushed pineapple
4 oz. chopped walnuts
3½ oz. coconut flakes

Mix together: flour, baking powder, baking soda, salt and cinnamon. Add sugar, oil and eggs. Beat well. Add carrots, pineapple (drained), nuts and coconut; blend thoroughly. Pour into a 9 x 13-inch greased and floured pan. Bake in preheated 350° oven for 35 to 40 minutes or until done. Cool and frost.

RUGLACH
(Pastry Crescents)

Jo Russo

Dough:

2 c. sifted all-purpose flour
1 c. (½ lb.) unsalted butter

8 oz. cream cheese

Filling:

⅓ c. sugar
1 T. cinnamon

½ c. chopped walnuts
¼-½ c. raisins

In mixing bowl, place flour, butter and cream cheese; mix well until dough forms. Divide into 4 balls of pastry. Wrap in plastic wrap or waxed paper and refrigerate at least 2 hours or longer. When ready, on floured board or pastry cloth, roll each piece of pastry into a ¼ inch thick round about 10 to 12 inches in diameter. In a small mixing bowl, mix together the sugar, cinnamon, nuts and raisins. Sprinkle this filling on each pastry round then cut each round into 12 wedges. Starting at wide end, roll up each wedge to a crescent. Place on greased cookie sheet. Bake in preheated 375° oven until brown, about 15 to 20 minutes. Yield: 4 dozen (approximately).

GLORIOUS GRAHAMS
(Cookies)

Lyn Fennel

½ lb. butter
½ c. sugar
1 tsp. vanilla
1 c. chopped nuts

Honey graham crackers
   (approximately 24 sq.)
Use jelly roll pan, approximately
   16 x 11 inches

(continued)

Arrange graham crackers in pan. Line up slits in crackers to make slicing easier. Melt butter and add sugar. Boil 2 minutes, stirring constantly. Remove from heat and add vanilla. **Work quickly.** Pour over graham crackers, smooth evenly. Sprinkle nuts over top. Bake in 350° oven for 10 minutes. Cool only 2 to 3 minutes. Cut into slices. Place on waxed paper to complete cooling.

EASY PEANUT CRUNCH COOKIES

Lorraine Modulick

½ c. peanut butter
1 (6-oz.) pkg. butterscotch
  morsels

2 c. chow mein noodles
Candied cherries

Combine in double boiler peanut butter and morsels. Stir until smooth. Add and stir in chow mein noodles. Coat thoroughly. Drop by teaspoonful onto a wax paper-lined cookie sheet. Top with a candied cherry. Chill until set.

PEANUT BUTTER CUPS

Jocelyn Stevens
Carol Leslie Feintuch

½ c. peanut butter
½ c. butter
½ c. sugar
½ c. brown sugar
1¼ c. flour
1 egg

½ tsp. vanilla
¾ tsp. baking powder
½ tsp. salt
14-oz. bag Reese's peanut
  butter cups (remove papers)

Cream butter, peanut butter, egg and vanilla. Add sugar, brown sugar, flour, baking powder and salt. Form dough into balls (48). Press into mini cup sheets (pans), make a thumb print. Bake at 375° for 8 to 10 minutes. Immediately put peanut butter cup into thumb print while in pans.

NUT CRUNCH COOKIES

Barbara Ryan

1 c. butter or margarine
½ c. sugar
1 tsp. vanilla

½ c. crushed potato chips
½ c. chopped pecans/walnuts
2 c. sifted flour

Cream butter or margarine, sugar and vanilla. Add crushed potato chips and nuts. Stir in flour. Form into small balls about 1 tablespoon each. Place on ungreased cookie sheet. Press flat with juice glass dipped in cinnamon/sugar. Bake at 350° for 16 to 18 minutes until lightly browned. Add sprinkles or colored crystals of desired.

34808-00

NO-BAKE COOKIES

Michelle James

2 c. sugar	4 T. butter
1/4 c. cocoa	1/2 c. peanut butter
1/2 c. + 1 T. milk	2 c. oatmeal

Mix in saucepan, sugar, cocoa, milk and butter. Bring to boil for 1 minute, then remove from heat. Add peanut butter and oatmeal. Drop on waxed oiled paper. Refrigerate.

ALMOND COOKIES

June Jorgensen

3/4 c. butter or margarine, softened	1 3/4 c. unsifted all-purpose flour
3/4 c. sugar	1/4 tsp. salt
1 whole egg	1 egg yolk
2 tsp. almond extract	1 T. water
	15 candied red cherries, halved

In large bowl, with portable mixer at medium speed, beat butter, sugar, whole egg and almond extract until very light and fluffy. On sheet of waxed paper, sift flour with baking soda and salt. Beat into butter mixture until well combined. Refrigerate, covered, 1 hour. Preheat oven to 350°. Using hands, form dough into 30 balls. Place on ungreased cookie sheet, 3 inches apart to allow for spreading; flatten with hands to 1/2-inch thickness. Using fork, beat egg yolk and water slightly; brush some over cookie tops. Firmly press cherry half in center of each. Brush again with egg yolk mixture. Bake 15 minutes or until light golden in color. Cool in wire rack. Makes approximately 2 1/2 dozen.

DANISH WEDDING RINGS

Pauline Bridge

1 c. butter	1/2 c. chopped nuts
1/2 c. powdered sugar	1 tsp. vanilla
2 c. sifted flour	1 lb. powdered sugar

Mix butter and sugar. Add flour, vanilla and nuts. Roll into balls the size of small walnuts. Bake 20 minutes at 350°. **Cool.** Shake in plastic bags with powdered sugar to coat well.

PECAN CRESCENT COOKIES

Laura Mondulick

1 c. butter (no substitutes), softened	1 tsp. vanilla
1/2 c. sugar	1 1/2 c. pecans, finely chopped
	Confectioners' sugar

(continued)

In a mixing bowl, cream butter, sugar and vanilla. Gradually add flour. Stir in pecans. Shape rounded teaspoonfuls of dough into 2½-inch logs and shape into crescents. Place 1 inch apart on ungreased baking sheets. Bake at 325° for 20 to 22 minutes or until set and bottoms are lightly browned. Let stand for 2 to 3 minutes before removing to wire racks to cool. Dust with confectioners' sugar before serving.

BLUEBERRY SQUARES

Pauline H. Vachon

3 c. flour
2 tsp. baking powder
1½ c. sugar
2 eggs, beaten

1 tsp. vanilla extract
2 sticks (1 c.) margarine or
  butter
2 c. fresh or frozen blueberries

Sift together flour, baking powder and sugar, set aside. Mix vanilla and eggs, then add to flour mixture. With a pastry blender, cut margarine or butter into flour mixture until crumbly. Press half of dough on bottom of 13 x 9-inch pan. Cover with 2 cups blueberries. Cover with remaining dough leaving crumbly. Bake at 350° for 40 to 50 minutes or until light golden.

FRUITFUL PARTY SQUARES

Angela Smith

1 c. muscats (raisins)
½ c. semi-sweet chocolate bits
½ c. chopped nuts
½ c. chopped maraschino
  cherries, well drained
1 c. plus 2 T. flour

⅓ c. margarine or butter
1½ c. brown sugar, well packed
2 eggs
1 tsp. vanilla
1 tsp. baking powder
½ tsp. salt

Chop raisins, combine with chocolate bits, nuts, cherries and 2 tablespoons flour. Cream butter and sugar until fluffy; beat in egg and vanilla. Blend in 1 cup flour, sifted with baking powder and salt; add raisin mixture. Spread in greased 9-inch square pan. Bake at 350° for about 35 minutes. Cool. Makes 36 squares.

JOCIE'S DOUBLE DELICIOUS BARS

Jocelyn Stevens

½ c. butter
1½ c. graham cracker crumbs
1 (14-oz.) can Eagle Brand
  sweetened condensed milk

1 (12-oz.) pkg. Toll House semi-
  sweet chocolate chips
1 c. Reese's peanut butter chips

Heat oven to 350° (325° for glass dish). In 13 x 9-inch baking pan, melt butter in oven. Sprinkle crumbs evenly over butter; pour sweetened

(continued)

112

34808-00

condensed milk evenly over crumbs. Top with chips; press down firmly. Bake 25 to 30 minutes or until lightly browned. Cool; cut into bars. Store loosely covered at room temperature.

NO-BAKE BREAKFAST BARS

Marie Marshall

1½ c. peanut butter
1 c. honey
¾ c. brown sugar

5 c. bran or oat flake dry cereal
1 c. dried fruit pieces or raisins

Combine peanut butter, honey and brown sugar in large saucepan. Bring to a boil, stirring constantly. Remove from heat; quickly stir in cereal and fruit; mix well. Using buttered spatula or waxed paper. Press mixture evenly into a 13 x 9 x 2-inch dish, sprayed with nonstick cooking spray. Cool 15 minutes before cutting. Makes 18 bars.

SPECIAL RICE KRISPY BARS

Ginny Orenstein

5 c. Rice Krispies
1 c. white Karo syrup
1 c. sugar
1 c. peanut butter

1-2 T. margarine
1 (8-oz.) pkg. chocolate chips
1 (8-oz.) pkg. butterscotch chips

Grease 10 x 13-inch pan with margarine. Measure Rice Krispies into large bowl; set aside. Combine Karo and sugar in medium saucepan. Just bring to a boil. Remove from heat. Add peanut butter. Pour over Rice Krispies. Blend together. Press into pan. Melt chocolate and butterscotch chips together. Spread over. Cut into squares.

DATE BARS

Robert J. Woyciechowski

1 c. sugar
3 lg. eggs
1 c. flour
1 tsp. baking powder
⅛ tsp. salt

½ tsp. allspice
1 tsp. vanilla
2 c. chopped dates
1 c. chopped nuts
Powdered sugar

Sift sugar and beat eggs. Blend until very light. Sift flour, baking powder, salt and allspice. Add vanilla. Beat until ingredients are well blended. Add chopped dates and chopped nuts. Pour batter into greased and floured 9 x 13-inch pan. Bake at 325° for 25 minutes. Cool and cut into bars and roll in powdered sugar.

PUDDIN' COOKIES

Robert J. Woyciechowski

2¼ c. flour
1 tsp. baking soda
1 c. (2 sticks) softened butter or margarine
¼ c. sugar
¾ c. packed light brown sugar

1 (3-oz.) pkg. instant vanilla pudding
1 tsp. vanilla
2 lg. eggs
1 (12-oz.) pkg. chocolate chips
1 c. nuts (opt.)

In separate bowl mix flour and baking soda; set aside. In large bowl, mix sugars, butter and pudding. Add eggs and vanilla. Slowly add flour mixture and mix well, then add chips and nuts. Use nonstick cookie sheet. Bake at 375° for 8 to 10 minutes.

PECAN BRITTLE
(Microwave)

JoAnne Dain

1 c. sugar
½ c. light corn syrup
1 c. pecan pieces

1 tsp. butter or margarine
1 tsp. vanilla extract
1 tsp. baking soda

Combine sugar and corn syrup in a 1½-quart microwave-safe bowl, stirring well. Microwave at **high** 4 minutes; stir in pecans. Microwave at **high** 5 to 7 minutes or until lightly browned. Stir in butter and vanilla; microwave 1 minute. Stir in soda until foamy. Pour mixture onto a lightly greased baking sheet; cool on pan on a wire rack. Break into pieces and store in an airtight container. Yield: ¾ pound.

CANDY BARK

Molly Lawson

1 c. butter (real)
1 c. brown sugar
Saltine crackers

Chocolate chips (approximately 2 c.) use more or less as you like

Spread saltines over a cookie sheet. Boil cup of butter and cup of sugar for 3 minutes. Pour mixture over crackers and bake for 7 minutes in a preheated oven at 350°. Remove and let stand 3 minutes. Pour chocolate chips over crackers and let soften. Using a spoon, spread chocolate over crackers. Refrigerate until hard. Remove and break off into pieces.

34808-00

FAILPROOF FUDGE

Rhonda Maule

2½ c. sugar
1 c. evaporated milk
1 T. butter
¼ tsp. salt

1 tsp. vanilla extract
1 c. marshmallow creme
8-oz. pkg. semi-sweet chocolate
¾ c. pecan pieces

Combine sugar, milk, butter and salt into saucepan. Bring to vigorous boil, stirring often. Reduce heat. Simmer 6 minutes. Place vanilla, marshmallow creme and chocolate in large bowl. Slowly add boiling syrup over marshmallow-chocolate mixture. Beat by hand until chocolate is melted. Stir in nuts. Pour in buttered 8-inch square pan. Chill until firm. Cut into squares. Makes 2 pounds.

PUPPY CHOW

Jocelyn Stevens

1 lg. box Crispix cereal
2 c. powdered sugar
1 c. peanut butter

1 stick butter
8-oz. bag chocolate chips

Melt butter in bowl along with chocolate chips. Stir in peanut butter while still hot. Pour over cereal in a very large bowl. Once all cereal is coated put mixture in 2 brown grocery bags that have been doubled. Add powdered sugar and shake. Store in airtight container.

Recipe Favorites

Recipe Favorites

34808-00

This & That

Helpful Hints

- To refinish antiques or revitalize wood, use equal parts of linseed oil, white vinegar and turpentine. Rub into the furniture or wood with a soft cloth and lots of elbow grease.

- To stop the ants in your pantry, seal off cracks where they are entering with putty or petroleum jelly. Also, try sprinkling red pepper on floors and counter tops.

- To fix sticking sliding doors, windows and drawers, rub wax along their tracks.

- To make a simple polish for copper bottom cookware, mix equal parts of flour and salt with vinegar to create a paste. Store the paste in the refrigerator.

- Applying baking soda on a damp sponge will remove starch deposits from an iron. Make sure the iron is cold and unplugged.

- Remove stale odors in the wash by adding baking soda.

- To clean Teflon™, combine 1 cup water, 2 tablespoons baking soda and ½ cup liquid bleach. Boil in stained pan for 5 to 10 minutes or until the stain disappears. Wash, rinse, dry and condition with oil before using the pan again.

- Corning Ware can be cleaned by filling it with water and dropping in two denture cleaning tablets. Let stand for 30 to 45 minutes.

- A little instant coffee will work wonders on your wood furniture. Just make a thick paste from instant coffee and a little water, and rub it into the nicks and scratches on your dark wood furniture. You'll be amazed at how new and beautiful those pieces will look.

- For a clogged shower head, boil it for 15 minutes in a mixture of ½ cup vinegar and 1 quart water.

- For a spicy aroma, toss dried orange or lemon rinds into the fireplace.

- Tin coffee cans make excellent freezer containers for cookies.

- Add raw rice to the salt shaker to keep the salt free-flowing.

- Ice cubes will help sharpen garbage disposal blades.

CRANBERRY CHUTNEY

Ellen Grabowski

12 oz. fresh cranberries, rinsed
Peel of 1 lemon, slivered
1 c. brown sugar
1 c. water
½ c. raisins
½ c. cider vinegar

1 med. onion, minced
1 tsp. salt
1 tsp. dry mustard
Pinch of cayenne pepper
½ c. ginger conserve or
  preserves

Mix all ingredients except ginger conserve in large saucepan. Cook over moderate heat, stirring often, until mixture begins to thicken and cranberries are tender. Remove pan from heat and stir in ginger conserve. Cool mixture at room temperature. Store in refrigerator.

FRESH CRANBERRY ORANGE RELISH

Laura Mondulick

4 c. fresh cranberries, washed &
  stemmed
2 unpeeled oranges, quartered
  with seeds removed
2 apples, quartered with seeds
  removed

1 lemon, quartered with seeds
  removed
2½ c. sugar

Grind cranberries, oranges, apples and lemon. Add sugar and mix well. Chill 24 hours.

SWEET TART PICKLES

Carole Leslie Feintuch

8 c. thinly sliced cucumbers
1 c. sliced onions
1 med. sliced green pepper
2 c. sugar

1 c. vinegar
1 tsp. celery seed
1 tsp. mustard seed
1 T. salt

Slice cucumbers, onions and peppers. Mix sugar, vinegar, celery seed, mustard seed in large bowl. Add vegetables and mix well to separate rings. Spoon into clean jars and pour remaining liquid evenly over them. Keep refrigerated. Makes about 3 pints.

HEALTHY HOMEMADE EASY THOUSAND ISLAND DRESSING

Leslie McQueen

1 c. mayonnaise
½ c. chili sauce

3 T. sweet pickle relish
1 hard-boiled egg

(continued)

Beat in blender or with electric mixer. Refrigerate 2 to 3 hours.

HONEY DRESSING FOR AVOCADO SALAD

Leslie McQueen

½ c. sugar	¼ tsp. paprika
1 tsp. dry mustard	¼ c. vinegar
1 tsp. salt	1 c. Wesson oil

Chill oil in refrigerator for 1 hour. Mix sugar, dry mustard, salt, paprika and vinegar. Chill 1 hour, stirring once or twice. Beat sugar mixture and add chilled oil very slowly, beating until thick. Keep in refrigerator until used. If sugar settles to bottom. Beat again before use. Keeps indefinitely.

STEAK MARINADE

Joan Racelis

¼ c. oil	⅛ tsp. garlic powder
¼ c. soy sauce	½ tsp. ground ginger
1 tsp. sugar	1 T. lemon juice

Mix all ingredients. Use as marinade for steak or chicken or pork.

BEER BATTER WITH EGG

Jane Goodrich

2 lg. eggs, separated	½ tsp. salt
½ c. beer	½ tsp. baking powder
½ c. flour	Additional flour for dredging

In large bowl combine the egg yolks, beer, flour, salt and baking powder. In the second bowl beat the egg whites until stiff. Fold them into the batter gently but thoroughly. Dredge the food to be fried in additional flour, dip it into the batter and let each piece drip off for a few seconds. Fry only a few pieces at a time and use a slotted spoon to turn when they rise to the surface.

FRYING BATTER FOR FISH

Leslie McQueen

1 c. Bisquick	¾ c. beer
1 egg	1 tsp. seasoning salt

Blend all ingredients, coat fish and fry in oil.

34808-00

MUSTARD SAUCE FOR STONE CRABS
(From Joe's Stone Crab Restaurant, Miami Beach)

Barbara Grossman

3½ tsp. Coleman's dry mustard
1 c. mayonnaise
2 tsp. Worcestershire

1 tsp. A.1. steak sauce
⅛ c. light cream
Pinch of salt

In bowl, combine mustard and mayonnaise, beat one minute. Add Worcestershire sauce and A.1. sauce. Thin to desired consistency with light cream. Add pinch of salt. Chill at least ½ hour. Makes 1 cup.

BIG MAC SAUCE

Leslie McQueen

1 c. Miracle Whip (NOT MAYONNAISE)
⅓ c. sweet pickle relish
¼ c. French dressing (orange color, NOT RED, PLEASE!)

1 T. sugar
½ tsp. dry minced onion
¼ tsp. black pepper

Mix together all ingredients and refrigerate.

SOUR CREAM RAISIN SAUCE
(For Ham)

Lorraine Mondulick

½ c. raisins
2 c. dairy sour cream
½ tsp. salt

1 T. horseradish
2 tsp. lemon juice

Soak raisins in boiling water and let stand for ten minutes. Drain well. Combine raisins, sour cream, salt, horseradish and lemon juice. Chill and serve with ham.

MOCK SOUR CREAM

JoAnne Dain

1 c. low-fat cottage cheese
2 T. lemon juice
2 T. low-fat mayonnaise

¼ c. buttermilk
Pinch of salt

Place cottage cheese, lemon juice, mayonnaise and buttermilk in blender and blend thoroughly until creamy smooth. Serve as sauce for vegetables, on baked potatoes and for dressing potato salad. Combine with Hidden Valley Ranch salad dressing mix for a low-fat delicious Ranch dressing.

MEATLESS GARDEN PRIMAVERA SAUCE

Martha Swift

2 c. each sliced zucchini, sliced
  mushrooms
1 c. sliced onion
½ c. julienne cut yellow bell
  peppers
2 T. olive oil
1 (29 oz.) Hunt's tomato sauce
1 (6 oz.) Hunt's tomato paste

¾ c. chicken broth
¼ c. each white wine & sliced
  black olives
2 T. Italian parsley
½ T. Italian seasoning
½ tsp. garlic salt
¼ tsp. pepper
1 lb. spaghetti

In stockpot sauté zucchini, mushrooms, onion and bell peppers in hot oil until tender. Meanwhile in medium bowl combine remaining ingredients except spaghetti, mix well. Add sauce mixture to vegetables. Bring sauce to oil, reduce heat and simmer 5 minutes. Serve over cooked spaghetti.

BAKED PINEAPPLE

Mary Button

1-lb. can crushed pineapple
2 T. flour
½ c. sugar

3 eggs
6 slices white bread
¼ lb. butter

Mix pineapple (do not drain) and eggs (slightly beaten) with flour and sugar. Cube 6 slices of bread. Melt butter and soak bread. Spread pineapple mixture in pan. Top with bread. Bake 30 minutes uncovered at 350°.

PINEAPPLE SURPRISE

Linda Kammerer

2 c. partially drained pineapple
2 c. grated cheddar cheese
5-6 T. flour

1 c. sugar
1 sleeve Ritz crackers
1 stick melted butter

Combine pineapple and cheddar cheese. Mix together flour and sugar. Mix with pineapple and cheese. Pour into 9 x 13-inch pan. Crumble crackers over top. Dribble butter over all. Bake at 350° for ½ hour.

MOCK CHEESE SOUFFLÉ

Mikki Gardner

8 slices bread, cubed without
  crust
1 lb. sharp cheddar cheese,
  grated

3 eggs, beaten well
2 c. milk
¼ c. melted butter

(continued)

34808-00

Grease a 2-quart casserole. Place ½ bread cubes and ½ of cheese. Repeat layer. End with cheese on top. Pour liquid all over. Sprinkle with paprika. Place in refrigerator overnight. Remove 2½ hours before baking. Bake at 350° for 1 hour. Let rise 10 minutes before serving.

SUNRISE SANDWICH

Leslie McQueen

1 (1-lb.) can Pillsbury Grands refrigerated buttermilk biscuits
8 slices bacon, crispy cooked & cut in half
1 T. margarine or butter
¼ c. chopped onion

¼ c. chopped green bell pepper
8 eggs
¼ tsp. salt
⅛ tsp. pepper
8 slices American cheese

Bake Pillsbury buttermilk biscuits as directed on the package; keep warm. Prepare 8 slices of bacon. Melt margarine in skillet over medium heat. Add bell pepper and onion cook and stir 2 minutes, until tender. Combine eggs, salt and pepper; blend well. Add to mixture in skillet. Cook until egg mixture is almost set but still moist, stirring occasionally. **To serve:** Split warm biscuits. Spoon egg mixture evenly onto bottom half of each biscuit. Top each half with cheese, bacon and remaining biscuit half.

BERRY BRUNCH SYRUP

Leslie McQueen

1 (12-oz.) jar seedless raspberry or strawberry jam
¼ c. "I Can't Believe It's Not Butter!" spread

2 tsp. sugar
1 tsp. grated orange peel (opt.)

In a 1-quart saucepan, melt jam, butter spread, sugar and orange peel over medium heat, stirring occasionally, until smooth. Serve over French toast, pancakes or waffles.

SWEET AND SALTY NUTS

Laura Mondulick

1 lb. walnuts or pecans
1 stick butter
2 egg whites

Salt to taste
1 c. brown sugar

Beat egg whites (no peaks). Add salt. Mix in brown sugar and nuts. Stir well. Melt butter in a 250° oven in a jelly roll pan. Add nut mixture to pan. Bake at 250° for 1 hour. Mix nuts every 15 minutes.

HUNGARIAN MACARONI

Julia Borsos

3 slices smoked bacon
¼ c. oil
1¾ c. onion
2 T. paprika
3½ c. veal

Salt & garlic
1 c. diced green pepper
1 sm. tomato
5 c. macaroni
1 c. grated cheese

Fry the bacon until it is translucent, add the chopped onion and fry until it is light brown. Add the paprika, then immediately add the meat which is cut approximately pea-size. Add salt and a small amount of garlic; if it loses its liquid, add a small amount of water. When the meat is almost done, add the green peppers and tomato cut into small cubes. Simmer until almost all of the liquid is used up. Cook the macaroni and add to the meat. Place the mixture in an ovenproof dish and sprinkle with cheese. Heat in oven for few minutes.

SOUP PASTA

Julia Borsos

¾ c. flour
1 egg

Pinch salt

Prepare a stiff dough from the flour and egg (no water). On a floured broad, roll out dough (thinly). With floured fingers pinch small fingernail-size pieces out. Add pieces to any boiling soup. Stir soup. Pasta is cooked when it comes to the surface, 2 to 3 minutes.

PINEAPPLE STUFFING

Maria Hutchinson

1 c. melted butter
2 c. sugar
2 (20-oz.) cans crushed
  pineapple, drained

8 eggs, beaten together
10 slices bread, cubed (remove
  the crust)

Mix all the above together and put into a greased casserole. Sprinkle the top with cinnamon. Bake 1 hour in a 325° oven.

CHOCOLATE MOUSSE FROSTING

Lorraine Mondulick

2 c. heavy cream
1 c. powdered sugar, sifted

½ c. sweet Hershey's cocoa
Pinch salt

Beat together all ingredients in cold mixing bowl. Let set in refrigerator covered ½ hour.

34808-00

CHOCOLATE SATIN FROSTING

Pauline Bridge

2½ (1-oz.) sq. unsweetened
  chocolate
3 c. sifted powdered sugar
2 T. hot water
1 tsp. vanilla

1 egg
½ c. melted margarine
¼ c. walnuts
½ tsp. cinnamon (opt.)

Melt chocolate (in double boiler or microwave) with electric mixer. Blend sugar, water, egg, margarine and vanilla. It will appear thin, but beat to spreading consistency.

CREAM CHEESE FROSTING

Marie Elene Bruno

2 (3-oz.) pkgs. cream cheese
½ c. softened margarine or
  butter

2 tsp. vanilla
4½-4¾ c. sifted powdered
  sugar

In a bowl beat together cream cheese, margarine or butter and vanilla until light and fluffy. Gradually add 2 cups powdered sugar, beating well. Gradually beat in enough remaining powdered sugar to make frosting of spreading consistency.

CARAMEL FROSTING

Michelle James

¼ c. butter
1 c. brown sugar, packed

¼ c. milk
2 c. confectioners' sugar

Melt butter in saucepan, add brown sugar, boil over low heat 2 minutes, stirring all the time. Add milk; keep stirring until mixture boils. Remove from heat and sifted sugar and beat well.

MY FAVORITE PIZZA

Ken Mondulick

1 lg. pizza
½ pepperoni

½ c. mushroom, onion &
  meatballs

Call favorite pizza parlor. Wait 20 minutes. Drive your car to establishment, or call for delivery. **Eat.**

Recipe Favorites

34808-00

INDEX OF CONTRIBUTORS

INDEX OF RECIPES

Main Dishes & Casseroles

Cakes, Cookies & Candy

This & That

How to Order

Get your additional copies of this cookbook by returning an order form and your check or money order to:

Lakewood Ranch Women's Club, Inc.
P.O. Box 21286
Bradenton, FL 34204
(941) 751-2510

Please send me _____ copies of the **Pleasures from the Good Earth** cookbook at **$13.00** per copy and **$4.00** for shipping and handling per book. Enclosed is my check or money order for $_____.

Mail Books To:

Name_____

Address _____

City _____ State _____ Zip _____

Please send me _____ copies of the **Pleasures from the Good Earth** cookbook at **$13.00** per copy and **$4.00** for shipping and handling per book. Enclosed is my check or money order for $_____.

Mail Books To:

Name_____

Address _____

City _____ State _____ Zip _____

34808-mu

Herbs & Spices

Marjoram   May be used both dried or green. Use to flavor fish, poultry, omelets, lamb, stew, stuffing and tomato juice.

Mint   Aromatic with a cool flavor. Excellent in beverages, fish, lamb, cheese, soup, peas, carrots, and fruit desserts.

Oregano   Strong, aromatic odor. Use whole or ground in tomato juice, fish, eggs, pizza, omelets, chili, stew, gravy, poultry and vegetables.

Paprika   A bright red pepper, this spice is used in meat, vegetables and soups or as a garnish for potatoes, salads or eggs.

Parsley   Best when used fresh, but can be used dried as a garnish or as a seasoning. Try in fish, omelets, soup, meat, stuffing and mixed greens.

Rosemary   Very aromatic. Can be used fresh or dried. Season fish, stuffing, beef, lamb, poultry, onions, eggs, bread and potatoes. Great in dressings.

Saffron   Orange-yellow in color, this spice flavors or colors foods. Use in soup, chicken, rice and breads.

Sage   Use fresh or dried. The flowers are sometimes used in salads. May be used in tomato juice, fish, omelets, beef, poultry, stuffing, cheese spreads and breads.

Tarragon   Leaves have a pungent, hot taste. Use to flavor sauces, salads, fish, poultry, tomatoes, eggs, green beans, carrots and dressings.

Thyme   Sprinkle leaves on fish or poultry before broiling or baking. Throw a few sprigs directly on coals shortly before meat is finished grilling.

Baking Breads

Hints for Baking Breads

1. Kneading dough for 30 seconds after mixing improves the texture of baking powder biscuits.

2. Instead of shortening, use cooking or salad oil in waffles and hot cakes.

3. When bread is baking, a small dish of water in the oven will help keep the crust from hardening.

4. Dip a spoon in hot water to measure shortening, butter, etc., and the fat will slip out more easily.

5. Small amounts of leftover corn may be added to pancake batter for variety.

6. To make bread crumbs, use the fine cutter of a food grinder and tie a large paper bag over the spout in order to prevent flying crumbs.

7. When you are doing any sort of baking, you get better results if you remember to preheat your cookie sheet, muffin tins or cake pans.

Rules for Use of Leavening Agents

1. In simple flour mixtures, use 2 teaspoons baking powder to leaven 1 cup flour. Reduce this amount 1/2 teaspoon for each egg used.

2. To 1 teaspoon soda use 2 1/4 teaspoons cream of tartar, 2 cups freshly soured milk, or 1 cup molasses.

3. To substitute soda and an acid for baking powder, divide the amount of baking powder by 4. Take that as your measure and add acid according to rule 2.

Proportions of Baking Powder to Flour

biscuits ....to 1 cup flour use 1 1/4 tsp. baking powder
cake with oil ....to 1 cup flour use 1 tsp. baking powder
muffins ....to 1 cup flour use 1 1/2 tsp. baking powder
popovers ....to 1 cup flour use 1 1/4 tsp. baking powder
waffles ....to 1 cup flour use 1 1/4 tsp. baking powder

Proportions of Liquid to Flour

drop batter ....to 1 cup liquid use 2 to 2 1/2 cups flour
pour batter ....to 1 cup liquid use 1 cup flour
soft dough ....to 1 cup liquid use 3 to 3 1/2 cups flour
stiff dough ....to 1 cup liquid use 4 cups flour

Time and Temperature Chart

Breads	Minutes	Temperature
biscuits	12 - 15	400° - 450°
cornbread	25 - 30	400° - 425°
gingerbread	40 - 50	350° - 370°
loaf	50 - 60	350° - 400°
nut bread	50 - 75	350°
popovers	30 - 40	425° - 450°
rolls	20 - 30	400° - 450°

Baking Desserts

Perfect Cookies

Cookie dough that is to be rolled is much easier to handle after it has been refrigerated for 10 to 30 minutes. This keeps the dough from sticking, even though it may be soft. If not done, the soft dough may require more flour and too much flour makes cookies hard and brittle. Place on a floured board only as much dough as can be easily managed. Flour the rolling pin slightly and roll lightly to desired thickness. Cut shapes close together and add trimmings to dough that needs to be rolled. Place pans or sheets in upper third of oven. Watch cookies carefully while baking in order to avoid burned edges. When sprinkling sugar on cookies, try putting it into a salt shaker in order to save time.

Perfect Pies

1. Pie crust will be better and easier to make if all the ingredients are cool.

2. The lower crust should be placed in the pan so that it covers the surface smoothly. Air pockets beneath the surface will push the crust out of shape while baking.

3. Folding the top crust over the lower crust before crimping will keep juices in the pie.

4. In making custard pie, bake at a high temperature for about ten minutes to prevent a soggy crust. Then finish baking at a low temperature.

5. When making cream pie, sprinkle crust with powdered sugar in order to prevent it from becoming soggy.

Perfect Cakes

1. Fill cake pans two-thirds full and spread batter into corners and sides, leaving a slight hollow in the center.

2. Cake is done when it shrinks from the sides of the pan or if it springs back when touched lightly with the finger.

3. After removing a cake from the oven, place it on a rack for about five minutes. Then, the sides should be loosened and the cake turned out on a rack in order to finish cooling.

4. Do not frost cakes until thoroughly cool.

5. Icing will remain where you put it if you sprinkle cake with powdered sugar first.

Time and Temperature Chart

Dessert	Time	Temperature
butter cake, layer	20-40 min.	380° - 400°
butter cake, loaf	40-60 min.	360° - 400°
cake, angel	50-60 min.	300° - 360°
cake, fruit	3-4 hrs.	275° - 325°
cake, sponge	40-60 min.	300° - 350°
cookies, molasses	18-20 min.	350° - 375°
cookies, thin	10-12 min.	380° - 390°
cream puffs	45-60 min.	300° - 350°
meringue	40-60 min.	250° - 300°
pie crust	20-40 min.	400° - 500°

Vegetables & Fruits

Vegetable	Cooking Method	Time
artichokes	boiled	40 min.
	steamed	45-60 min.
asparagus tips	boiled	10-15 min.
beans, lima	boiled	20-40 min.
	steamed	60 min.
beans, string	boiled	15-35 min.
	steamed	60 min.
beets, old	boiled or steamed	1-2 hours
beets, young with skin	boiled	30 min.
	steamed	60 min.
	baked	70-90 min.
broccoli, flowerets	boiled	5-10 min.
broccoli, stems	boiled	20-30 min.
brussels sprouts	boiled	20-30 min.
cabbage, chopped	boiled	10-20 min.
	steamed	25 min.
carrots, cut across	boiled	8-10 min.
	steamed	40 min.
cauliflower, flowerets	boiled	8-10 min.
cauliflower, stem down	boiled	20-30 min.
corn, green, tender	boiled	5-10 min.
	steamed	15 min.
	baked	20 min.
corn on the cob	boiled	8-10 min.
	steamed	15 min.
eggplant, whole	boiled	30 min.
	steamed	40 min.
	baked	45 min.
parsnips	boiled	25-40 min.
	steamed	60 min.
	baked	60-75 min.
peas, green	boiled or steamed	5-15 min.
potatoes	boiled	20-40 min.
	steamed	60 min.
	baked	45-60 min.
pumpkin or squash	boiled	20-40 min.
	steamed	45 min.
	baked	60 min.
tomatoes	boiled	5-15 min.
turnips	boiled	25-40 min.

Drying Time Table

Fruit	Sugar or Honey	Cooking Time
apricots	1/4 c. for each cup of fruit	about 40 min.
figs	1 T. for each cup of fruit	about 30 min.
peaches	1/4 c. for each cup of fruit	about 45 min.
prunes	2 T. for each cup of fruit	about 45 min.

Vegetables & Fruits

Buying Fresh Vegetables

Artichokes: Look for compact, tightly closed heads with green, clean-looking leaves. Avoid those with leaves that are brown or separated.

Asparagus: Stalks should be tender and firm; tips should be close and compact. Choose the stalks with very little white; they are more tender. Use asparagus soon because it toughens rapidly.

Beans, Snap: Those with small seeds inside the pods are best. Avoid beans with dry-looking pods.

Broccoli, Brussels Sprouts and Cauliflower: Flower clusters on broccoli and cauliflower should be tight and close together. Brussels sprouts should be firm and compact. Smudgy, dirty spots may indicate pests or disease.

Cabbage and Head Lettuce: Choose heads that are heavy for their size. Avoid cabbage with worm holes and lettuce with discoloration or soft rot.

Cucumbers: Choose long, slender cucumbers for best quality. May be dark or medium green, but yellow ones are undesirable.

Mushrooms: Caps should be closed around the stems. Avoid black or brown gills.

Peas and Lima Beans: Select pods that are well-filled but not bulging. Avoid dried, spotted, yellow, or flabby pods.

Buying Fresh Fruits

Bananas: Skin should be free of bruises and black or brown spots. Purchase them green and allow them to ripen at home at room temperature.

Berries: Select plump, solid berries with good color. Avoid stained containers which indicate wet or leaky berries. Berries with clinging caps, such as blackberries and raspberries, may be unripe. Strawberries without caps may be overripe.

Melons: In cantaloupes, thick, close netting on the rind indicates best quality. Cantaloupes are ripe when the stem scar is smooth and the space between the netting is yellow or yellow-green. They are best when fully ripe with fruity odor.

Honeydews are ripe when rind has creamy to yellowish color and velvety texture. Immature honeydews are whitish-green.

Ripe watermelons have some yellow color on one side. If melons are white or pale green on one side, they are not ripe.

Oranges, Grapefruit and Lemons: Choose those heavy for their size. Smoother, thinner skins usually indicate more juice. Most skin markings do not affect quality. Oranges with a slight greenish tinge may be just as ripe as fully colored ones. Light or greenish-yellow lemons are more tart than deep yellow ones. Avoid citrus fruits showing withered, sunken or soft areas.

Napkin Folding

General Tips:
Use well-starched linen napkins if possible. For more complicated folds, 24-inch napkins work best. Practice the folds with newspapers. Children can help. Once they learn the folds, they will have fun!

Shield

Easy fold. Elegant with monogram in corner.

1, 2

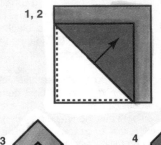

3

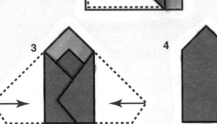

4

Instructions:
1. Fold into quarter size. If monogrammed, ornate corner should face down.
2. Turn up folded corner three-quarters.
3. Overlap right side and left side points.
4. Turn over; adjust sides so that they are even, single point in center.
5. Place point up or down on plate, or left of plate.

Rosette

Elegant on plate.

Instructions:
1. Fold left and right edges to center, leaving ½" opening along center.
2. Pleat firmly from top edge to bottom edge. Sharpen edges with hot iron.
3. Pinch center together. If necessary, use small piece of pipe cleaner to secure and top with single flower.
4. Spread out rosette.

1

2

3

4

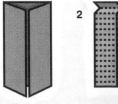

Napkin Folding

Candle

Easy to do; can be decorated.

Instructions:
1. Fold into triangle, point at top.
2. Turn lower edge up 1".
3. Turn over, folded edge down.
4. Roll tightly from left to right.
5. Tuck in corner. Stand upright.

Fan

Pretty in napkin ring or on plate.

Instructions:
1. Fold top and bottom edges to center.
2. Fold top and bottom edges to center a second time.
3. Pleat firmly from the left edge. Sharpen edges with hot iron.
4. Spread out fan. Balance flat folds of each side on table. Well-starched napkins will hold shape.

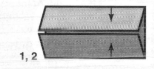

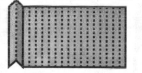

Lily

Effective and pretty on table.

Instructions:
1. Fold napkin into quarters.
2. Fold into triangle, closed corner to open points.
3. Turn two points over to other side. (Two points are on either side of closed point.)
4. Pleat.
5. Place closed end in glass. Pull down two points on each side and shape.

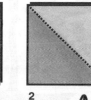

Measurements & Substitutions

Measurements

a pinch	1/8 teaspoon or less
3 teaspoons	1 tablespoon
4 tablespoons	1/4 cup
8 tablespoons	1/2 cup
12 tablespoons	3/4 cup
16 tablespoons	1 cup
2 cups	1 pint
4 cups	1 quart
4 quarts	1 gallon
8 quarts	1 peck
4 pecks	1 bushel
16 ounces	1 pound
32 ounces	1 quart
1 ounce liquid	2 tablespoons
8 ounces liquid	1 cup

**Use standard measuring spoons and cups.
All measurements are level.**

Substitutions

Ingredient	Quantity	Substitute
baking powder	1 teaspoon	1/4 tsp. baking soda plus 1/2 tsp. cream of tartar
catsup or chili sauce	1 cup	1 c. tomato sauce plus 1/2 c. sugar and 2 T. vinegar (for use in cooking)
chocolate	1 square (1 oz.)	3 or 4 T. cocoa plus 1 T. butter
cornstarch	1 tablespoon	2 T. flour or 2 tsp. quick-cooking tapioca
cracker crumbs	3/4 cup	1 c. bread crumbs
dates	1 lb.	1 1/2 c. dates, pitted and cut
dry mustard	1 teaspoon	1 T. prepared mustard
flour, self-rising	1 cup	1 c. all-purpose flour, 1/2 tsp. salt, and 1 tsp. baking powder
herbs, fresh	1 tablespoon	1 tsp. dried herbs
milk, sour	1 cup	1 T. lemon juice or vinegar plus sweet milk to make 1 c. (let stand 5 minutes)
whole	1 cup	1/2 c. evaporated milk plus 1/2 c. water
min. marshmallows	10	1 lg. marshmallow
onion, fresh	1 small	1 T. instant minced onion, rehydrated
sugar, brown	1/2 cup	2 T. molasses in 1/2 c. granulated sugar
powdered	1 cup	1 c. granulated sugar plus 1 tsp. cornstarch
tomato juice	1 cup	1/2 c. tomato sauce plus 1/2 c. water

**When substituting cocoa for chocolate in cakes, the amount of flour must
be reduced. Brown and white sugars usually can be interchanged.**

Equivalency Chart

Food	Quantity	Yield
apple	1 medium	1 cup
banana, mashed	1 medium	1/3 cup
bread	1 1/2 slices	1 cup soft crumbs
bread	1 slice	1/4 cup fine, dry crumbs
butter	1 stick or 1/4 pound	1/2 cup
cheese, American, cubed	1 pound	2 2/3 cups
American, grated	1 pound	5 cups
cream cheese	3-ounce package	6 2/3 tablespoons
chocolate, bitter	1 square	1 ounce
cocoa	1 pound	4 cups
coconut	1 1/2 pound package	2 2/3 cups
coffee, ground	1 pound	5 cups
cornmeal	1 pound	3 cups
cornstarch	1 pound	3 cups
crackers, graham	14 squares	1 cup fine crumbs
saltine	28 crackers	1 cup fine crumbs
egg	4-5 whole	1 cup
whites	8-10	1 cup
yolks	10-12	1 cup
evaporated milk	1 cup	3 cups whipped
flour, cake, sifted	1 pound	4 1/2 cups
rye	1 pound	5 cups
white, sifted	1 pound	4 cups
white, unsifted	1 pound	3 3/4 cups
gelatin, flavored	3 1/4 ounces	1/2 cup
unflavored	1/4 ounce	1 tablespoon
lemon	1 medium	3 tablespoon juice
marshmallows	16	1/4 pound
noodles, cooked	8-ounce package	7 cups
uncooked	4 ounces (1 1/2 cups)	2-3 cups cooked
macaroni, cooked	8-ounce package	6 cups
macaroni, uncooked	4 ounces (1 1/4 cups)	2 1/4 cups cooked
spaghetti, uncooked	7 ounces	4 cups cooked
nuts, chopped	1/4 pound	1 cup
almonds	1 pound	3 1/2 cups
walnuts, broken	1 pound	3 cups
walnuts, unshelled	1 pound	1 1/2 to 1 3/4 cups
onion	1 medium	1/2 cup
orange	3-4 medium	1 cup juice
raisins	1 pound	3 1/2 cups
rice, brown	1 cup	4 cups cooked
converted	1 cup	3 1/2 cups cooked
regular	1 cup	3 cups cooked
wild	1 cup	4 cups cooked
sugar, brown	1 pound	2 1/2 cups
powdered	1 pound	3 1/2 cups
white	1 pound	2 cups
vanilla wafers	22	1 cup fine crumbs
zwieback, crumbled	4	1 cups

Food Quantities
For Large Servings

	25 Servings	50 Servings	100 Servings
Beverages:			
coffee	½ pound and 1 ½ gallons water	1 pound and 3 gallons water	2 pounds and 6 gallons water
lemonade	10-15 lemons and 1 ½ gallons water	20-30 lemons and 3 gallons water	40-60 lemons and 6 gallons water
tea	1/12 pound and 1 ½ gallons water	1/6 pound and 3 gallons water	1/3 pound and 6 gallons water
Desserts:			
layered cake	1 12" cake	3 10" cakes	6 10" cakes
sheet cake	1 10" x 12" cake	1 12" x 20" cake	2 12" x 20" cakes
watermelon	37 ½ pounds	75 pounds	150 pounds
whipping cream	¾ pint	1 ½ to 2 pints	3-4 pints
Ice cream:			
brick	3 ¼ quarts	6 ½ quarts	13 quarts
bulk	2 ¼ quarts	4 ½ quarts or 1 ¼ gallons	9 quarts or 2 ½ gallons
Meat, poultry or fish:			
fish	13 pounds	25 pounds	50 pounds
fish, fillets or steak	7 ½ pounds	15 pounds	30 pounds
hamburger	9 pounds	18 pounds	35 pounds
turkey or chicken	13 pounds	25 to 35 pounds	50 to 75 pounds
wieners (beef)	6 ½ pounds	13 pounds	25 pounds
Salads, casseroles:			
baked beans	¾ gallon	1 ¼ gallons	2 ½ gallons
jello salad	¾ gallon	1 ¼ gallons	2 ½ gallons
potato salad	4 ¼ quarts	2 ¼ gallons	4 ½ gallons
scalloped potatoes	4 ½ quarts or 1 12" x 20" pan	9 quarts or 2 ¼ gallons	18 quarts 4 ½ gallons
spaghetti	1 ¼ gallons	2 ½ gallons	5 gallons
Sandwiches:			
bread	50 slices or 3 1-pound loaves	100 slices or 6 1-pound loaves	200 slices or 12 1-pound loaves
butter	½ pound	1 pound	2 pounds
lettuce	1 ½ heads	3 heads	6 heads
mayonnaise	1 cup	2 cups	4 cups
mixed filling			
meat, eggs, fish	1 ½ quarts	3 quarts	6 quarts
jam, jelly	1 quart	2 quarts	4 quarts

Microwave Hints

1. Place an open box of hardened brown sugar in the microwave oven with 1 cup hot water. Microwave on high for 1 1/2 to 2 minutes for 1/2 pound or 2 to 3 minutes for 1 pound.

2. Soften hard ice cream by microwaving at 30% power. One pint will take 15 to 30 seconds; one quart, 30-45 seconds; and one-half gallon, 45-60 seconds.

3. To melt chocolate, place 1/2 pound in glass bowl or measuring cup. Melt uncovered at 50% power for 3-4 minutes; stir after 2 minutes.

4. Soften one 8-ounce package of cream cheese by microwaving at 30% power for 2 to 2 1/2 minutes. One 3-ounce package of cream cheese will soften in 1 1/2 to 2 minutes.

5. A 4 1/2 ounce carton of whipped topping will thaw in 1 minute on the defrost setting. Whipped topping should be slightly firm in the center, but it will blend well when stirred. Do not over thaw!

6. Soften jello that has set up too hard - perhaps you were to chill it until slightly thickened and forgot it. Heat on a low power setting for a very short time.

7. Heat hot packs. A wet fingertip towel will take about 25 seconds. It depends on the temperature of the water used to wet the towel.

8. To scald milk, cook 1 cup for 2 to 2 1/2 minutes, stirring once each minute.

9. To make dry bread crumbs, cut 6 slices of bread into 1/2-inch cubes. Microwave in 3-quart casserole 6-7 minutes, or until dry, stirring after 3 minutes. Crush in blender.

10. Refresh stale potato chips, crackers or other snacks of such type by putting a plateful in the microwave for 30-45 seconds. Let stand for 1 minute to crisp. Cereals can also be crisped.

11. Nuts will be easier to shell if you place 2 cups of nuts in a 1-quart casserole with 1 cup of water. Cook for 4 to 5 minutes and the nutmeats will slip out whole after cracking the shell.

12. Stamp collectors can place a few drops of water on a stamp to remove it from an envelope. Heat in the microwave for 20 seconds, and the stamp will come off.

13. Using a round dish instead of a square one eliminates overcooked corners in baking cakes.

14. Sprinkle a layer of medium, finely chopped walnuts evenly onto the bottom and side of a ring pan or bundt cake pan to enhances the looks and eating quality. Pour in batter and microwave as recipe directs.

15. Do not salt foods on the surface as it causes dehydration and toughens food. Salt after you remove from the oven unless the recipe calls for using salt in the mixture.

16. Heat left-over custard and use it as frosting for a cake.

17. Melt marshmallow cream. Half of a 7-ounce jar will melt in 35-40 seconds on high. Stir to blend.

18. To toast coconut, spread 1/2 cup coconut in a pie plate and cook for 3-4 minutes, stirring every 30 seconds after 2 minutes. Watch closely, as it quickly browns.

19. To melt crystallized honey, heat uncovered jar on high for 30-45 seconds. If jar is large, repeat.

20. One stick of butter or margarine will soften in 1 minute when microwaved at 20% power.

Calorie Counter

Beverages

apple juice, 6 oz. 90
coffee (black) 0
cola type, 12 oz. 115
cranberry juice, 6 oz. 115
ginger ale, 12 oz. 115
grape juice, (prepared from
   frozen concentrate), 6 oz. 142
lemonade, (prepared from
   frozen concentrate), 6 oz. 85
milk, protein fortified, 1 c. 105
   skim, 1 c. 90
   whole, 1 c. 160
orange juice, 6 oz. 85
pineapple juice, unsweetened, 6 oz. 95
root beer, 12 oz. 150
tonic (quinine water) 12 oz. 132

Breads

cornbread, 1 sm. square 130
dumplings, 1 med. 70
French toast, 1 slice..........................135
melba toast, 1 slice 25
muffins, blueberry, 1 muffin 110
   bran, 1 muffin...............................106
   corn, 1 muffin................................125
   English, 1 muffin 280
pancakes, 1 (4-in.) 60
pumpernickel, 1 slice 75
rye, 1 slice 60
waffle, 1 216
white, 1 slice 60-70
whole wheat, 1 slice 55-65

Cereals

cornflakes, 1 c....................................105
cream of wheat, 1 c. 120
oatmeal, 1 c. 148
rice flakes, 1 c. 105
shredded wheat, 1 biscuit 100
sugar krisps, ¾ c...............................110

Crackers

graham, 1 cracker............................15-30
rye crisp, 1 cracker...............................35
saltine, 1 cracker..............................17-20
wheat thins, 1 cracker 9

Dairy Products

butter or margarine, 1 T....................100
cheese, American, 1 oz....................100
   camembert, 1 oz. 85
   cheddar, 1 oz. 115
   cottage cheese, 1 oz. 30
   mozzarella, 1 oz. 90
   parmesan, 1 oz. 130
   ricotta, 1 oz.....................................50
   roquefort, 1 oz. 105
   Swiss, 1 oz. 105
cream, light, 1 T. 30
   heavy, 1 T. 55
   sour, 1 T. 45
hot chocolate, with milk, 1 c. 277
milk chocolate, 1 oz. 145-155
yogurt
   made w/ whole milk, 1 c. 150-165
   made w/ skimmed milk, 1 c. 125

Eggs

fried, 1 lg. 100
poached or boiled, 1 lg. 75-80
scrambled or in omelet, 1 lg. 110-130

Fish and Seafood

bass, 4 oz. 105
salmon, broiled or baked, 3 oz. 155
sardines, canned in oil, 3 oz. 170
trout, fried, 3 ½ oz. 220
tuna, in oil, 3 oz. 170
   in water, 3 oz. 110

Calorie Counter

Fruits

apple, 1 med. 80-100
applesauce, sweetened, ½ c. 90-115
   unsweetened, ½ c...........................50
banana, 1 med. 85
blueberries, ½ c................................45
cantaloupe, ½ c.................................24
cherries (pitted), raw, ½ c. 40
grapefruit, ½ med. 55
grapes, ½ c. 35-55
honeydew, ½ c. 55
mango, 1 med. 90
orange, 1 med. 65-75
peach, 1 med. 35
pear, 1 med. 60-100
pineapple, fresh, ½ c.......................40
   canned in syrup, ½ c. 95
plum, 1 med. 30
strawberries, fresh, ½ c...................30
   frozen and sweetened, ½ c. 120-140
tangerine, 1 lg. 39
watermelon, ½ c. 42

Meat and Poultry

beef, ground (lean), 3 oz. 185
   roast, 3 oz. 185
chicken, broiled, 3 oz 115
lamb chop (lean), 3 oz. 175-200
steak, sirloin, 3 oz. 175
   tenderloin, 3 oz. 174
   top round, 3 oz. 162
turkey, dark meat, 3 oz. 175
   white meat, 3 oz. 150
veal, cutlet, 3 oz.............................156
   roast, 3 oz. 76

Nuts

almonds, 2 T. 105
cashews, 2 T. 100
peanuts, 2 T. 105
peanut butter, 1 T.............................95
pecans, 2 T. 95
pistachios, 2 T. 92
walnuts, 2 T. 80

Pasta

macaroni or spaghetti,
   cooked, ¾ c. 115

Salad Dressings

blue cheese, 1 T. 70
French, 1 T.......................................65
Italian, 1 T. 80
mayonnaise, 1 T. 100
olive oil, 1 T. 124
Russian, 1 T. 70
salad oil, 1 T...................................120

Soups

bean, 1 c. 130-180
beef noodle, 1 c. 70
bouillon and consomme, 1 c. 30
chicken noodle, 1 c. 65
chicken with rice, 1 c. 50
minestrone, 1 c................................80-150
split pea, 1 c. 145-170
tomato with milk, 1 c. 170
vegetable, 1 c................................80-100

Vegetables

asparagus, 1 c....................................35
broccoli, cooked, ½ c. 25
cabbage, cooked, ½ c. 15-20
carrots, cooked, ½ c. 25-30
cauliflower, ½ c. 10-15
corn (kernels), ½ c. 70
green beans, 1 c. 30
lettuce, shredded, ½ c.......................5
mushrooms, canned, ½ c. 20
onions, cooked, ½ c. 30
peas, cooked, ½ c...............................60
potato, baked, 1 med. 90
   chips, 8-10 100
   mashed, w/milk & butter, 1 c. ..200-300
spinach, 1 c......................................40
tomato, raw, 1 med. 25
   cooked, ½ c. 30

Cooking Terms

Au gratin: Topped with crumbs and/or cheese and browned in oven or under broiler.

Au jus: Served in its own juices.

Baste: To moisten foods during cooking with pan drippings or special sauce in order to add flavor and prevent drying.

Bisque: A thick cream soup.

Blanch: To immerse in rapidly boiling water and allow to cook slightly.

Cream: To soften a fat, especially butter, by beating it at room temperature. Butter and sugar are often creamed together, making a smooth, soft paste.

Crimp: To seal the edges of a two-crust pie either by pinching them at intervals with the fingers or by pressing them together with the tines of a fork.

Crudites: An assortment of raw vegetables (i.e. carrots, broccoli, celery, mushrooms) that is served as an hors d'oeuvre, often accompanied by a dip.

Degrease: To remove fat from the surface of stews, soups, or stock. Usually cooled in the refrigerator so that fat hardens and is easily removed.

Dredge: To coat lightly with flour, cornmeal, etc.

Entree: The main course.

Fold: To incorporate a delicate substance, such as whipped cream or beaten egg whites, into another substance without releasing air bubbles. A spatula is used to gently bring part of the mixture from the bottom of the bowl to the top. The process is repeated, while slowly rotating the bowl, until the ingredients are thoroughly blended.

Glaze: To cover with a glossy coating, such as a melted and somewhat diluted jelly for fruit desserts.

Julienne: To cut vegetables, fruits, or cheeses into match-shaped slivers.

Marinate: To allow food to stand in a liquid in order to tenderize or to add flavor.

Meuniére: Dredged with flour and sautéed in butter.

Mince: To chop food into very small pieces.

Parboil: To boil until partially cooked; to blanch. Usually final cooking in a seasoned sauce follows this procedure.

Pare: To remove the outermost skin of a fruit or vegetable.

Poach: To cook gently in hot liquid kept just below the boiling point.

Purée: To mash foods by hand by rubbing through a sieve or food mill, or by whirling in a blender or food processor until perfectly smooth.

Refresh: To run cold water over food that has been parboiled in order to stop the cooking process quickly.

Sauté: To cook and/or brown food in a small quantity of hot shortening.

Scald: To heat to just below the boiling point, when tiny bubbles appear at the edge of the saucepan.

Simmer: To cook in liquid just below the boiling point. The surface of the liquid should be barely moving, broken from time to time by slowly rising bubbles.

Steep: To let food stand in hot liquid in order to extract or to enhance flavor, like tea in hot water or poached fruit in sugar syrup.

Toss: To combine ingredients with a repeated lifting motion.

Whip: To beat rapidly in order to incorporate air and produce expansion, as in heavy cream or egg whites.

Cooking Tips

1. After stewing a chicken, cool in broth before cutting into chunks; It will have twice the flavor.

2. To slice meat into thin strips, as for stir-fry dishes, partially freeze it so it will slice more easily.

3. A roast with the bone in will cook faster than a boneless roast. The bone carries the heat to the inside more quickly.

4. When making a roast, place dry onion soup mix in the bottom of your roaster pan. After removing the roast, add 1 can of mushroom soup and you will have a good brown gravy.

5. For a juicier hamburger, add cold water to the beef before grilling (½ cup to 1 pound of meat).

6. To freeze meatballs, place them on a cookie sheet until frozen. Place in plastic bags. They will stay separated so that you may remove as many as you want.

7. To keep cauliflower white while cooking, add a little milk to the water.

8. When boiling corn, add sugar to the water instead of salt. Salt will toughen the corn

9. To ripen tomatoes, put them in a brown paper bag in a dark pantry, and they will ripen overnight.

10. To keep celery crisp, stand it upright in a pitcher of cold, salted water and refrigerate.

11. When cooking cabbage, place a small tin cup or can half full of vinegar on the stove near the cabbage. It will absorb the odor.

12. Potatoes soaked in salt water for 20 minutes before baking will bake more rapidly.

13. Let raw potatoes stand in cold water for at least a half-hour before frying in order to improve the crispness of French-fried potatoes. Dry potatoes thoroughly before adding to oil.

14. Use greased muffin tins as molds when baking stuffed green peppers.

15. A few drops of lemon juice in the water will whiten boiled potatoes.

16. Buy mushrooms before they "open." When stems and caps are attached firmly, mushrooms are truly fresh.

17. Do not use metal bowls when mixing salads. Use wood, glass or china.

18. Lettuce keeps better if you store it in the refrigerator without washing it. Keep the leaves dry. Wash lettuce the day you are going to use it.

19. Do not use soda to keep vegetables green. It destroys Vitamin C.

20. Do not despair if you oversalt gravy. Stir in some instant mashed potatoes to repair the damage. Just add a little more liquid in order to offset the thickening.

Herbs & Spices

Acquaint yourself with herbs and spices. Add in small amounts, ¼ teaspoon for every 4 servings. Crush dried herbs or snip fresh ones before using. Use 3 times more fresh herbs if substituting fresh for dried.

Basil
Sweet, warm flavor with an aromatic odor. Use whole or ground. Good with lamb, fish, roast, stews, ground beef, vegetables, dressing and omelets.

Bay Leaves
Pungent flavor. Use whole leaf but remove before serving. Good in vegetable dishes, seafood, stews and pickles.

Caraway
Spicy taste and aromatic smell. Use in cakes, breads, soups, cheese and sauerkraut.

Chives
Sweet, mild flavor like that of onion. Excellent in salads, fish, soups and potatoes.

Cilantro
Use fresh. Excellent in salads, fish, chicken, rice, beans and Mexican dishes.

Curry Powder
Spices are combined to proper proportions to give a distinct flavor to meat, poultry, fish and vegetables.

Dill
Both seeds and leaves are flavorful. Leaves may be used as a garnish or cooked with fish, soup, dressings, potatoes and beans. Leaves or the whole plant may be used to flavor pickles.

Fennel
Sweet, hot flavor. Both seeds and leaves are used. Use in small quantities in pies and baked goods. Leaves can be boiled with fish.

Ginger
A pungent root, this aromatic spice is sold fresh, dried or ground. Use in pickles, preserves, cakes, cookies, soups and meat dishes.

Publish Your Own Cookbook

We have the right ingredients...

Churches, schools, organizations, and families can preserve their favorite recipes by publishing a personalized cookbook. Cookbooks make a great **fundraiser** because they are easy to sell and highly profitable. Looking for a unique **keepsake**? Our low cost makes cookbooks affordable. "You supply the recipes and we'll do the rest!"™ COOKBOOKS BY MORRIS PRESS has 65 years of experience and an easy step-by-step program offering:

- ♥ 200 minimum order; as low as $1.65/book.
- ♥ Fast delivery, 90 days to pay, and guaranteed sales!
- ♥ Soft cover, hardback, or 3-ring style cookbooks.
- ♥ Many free features and options.

Mail the postage paid card, or for faster service:

- ♥ Visit our web site at www.morriscookbooks.com
- ♥ Call us at 1-800-445-6621, ext. CB

Discover the right ingredients for a really great cookbook.

Complete the information below, mail this card, and we'll send you our **FREE** *Guide to Publishing Your Own Cookbook.*

3212 E. Hwy 30
Kearney, NE 68847
800-445-6621

Name _____

Organization _____

Address _____

City _____ State _____ Zip _____

Phone (_____) _____

Publish Your Own Cookbook

❤   ❤   ❤   ❤   ❤   ❤

Cookbooks by Morris Press has the right ingredients to make a really great cookbook. "You supply the recipes and we'll do the rest!"™ Write us, call us, or contact us at our web site, and we'll send you our **FREE** step-by-step *Guide to Publishing Your Own Cookbook*. It's so easy.

Several ways to contact us:
- ❤ Return the **postage paid reply card** from the other side
- ❤ Order from our web site at **www.morriscookbooks.com**
- ❤ Call us at **1-800-445-6621, ext. CB**